Drunken Driving and the Law

MARK DE BLÁCAM
MA, Barrister-at-Law

SECOND EDITION

THE ROUND HALL PRESS
DUBLIN

This book was typeset in Ehrhardt 11 pt on 13 pt by
Gilbert Gough Typesetting, Dublin, for
THE ROUND HALL PRESS LTD
KIll Lane, Blackrock, Co. Dublin, Ireland
and in North America for
THE ROUND HALL PRESS LTD
c.o ISBS, 5804 NE Hassalo St, Portland, Oregon 97213.

© Mark de Blácam 1995

ISBN 1-85800-047-5

A catalogue record for this book is
available from the British Library.

First edition 1986
Reprinted 1991
Second edition 1995

Printed in Ireland by
Colour Books Ltd, Dublin

For my parents

Preface to the second edition

Many changes have taken place in the law relating to drunken driving since the publication of the first edition of this book nine years ago in 1986. The second edition attempts to take account of those changes and to state the law as of 1 June 1995. Many people helped me in different ways in preparing this edition. My thanks are due to Carol O'Farrell, Roderick McGilligan and William Penrose. I also thank Adrienne Cawley, Pádraig Dwyer, Paul Greene and Raghnal O'Riordan who helped with the proofreading. As in 1986 Michael Adams skilfully shepherded the book through to publication, and Kevin Haugh kindly took time to read the proofs and saved me from more mistakes than I care to acknowledge. But again, as in 1986, my greatest debt is due to my wife, Máire.

Contents

PREFACE vii

TABLE OF CASES xi

TABLE OF STATUTES xix

1   An Historical Introduction   1

2   Drunken Driving, Drunk in Charge and Related Offences   11

3   The Statutory Procedure in Drunken Driving Cases: Part 1   27

4   The Statutory Procedure in Drunken Driving Cases: Part 2   46

5   The Doctor's Form, the Bureau's Certificate and the
    Designated Doctor   65

6   Penalties   72

7   The Commencement of Charges   81

8   The Hearing   99

9   Appeals and other Review Procedures   111

APPENDICES 121

INDEX 141

Table of Cases

Attorney General v. Greene (1952) 86 ILTR 31 .... 6.04
Attorney General v. Healy [1928] IR 460 .... 7.01
Attorney General v. Hollingsworth (1973) 107 ILTR 77 .... 1.11
Attorney General v. McLoughlin [1931] IR 430 .... 9.07
Attorney General v. Mallen [1957] IR 344 .... 8.12
Attorney General (Crotty) v. O'Keeffe [1955] IR 24 .... 2.04
Attorney General (Doyle) v. Farrell (1954) 88 ILTR 174 .... 2.15
Attorney General (Enright) v. Reilly, unreported, High Court, 30
  January 1967 .... 2.06
Attorney General (Fahy) v. Bruen [1936] IR 750; (1936) 70 ILTR 247 ... 9.06
Attorney General (Lambe) v. Fitzgerald [1973] IR 195 .... 9.03
Attorney General (McDonnell) v. Higgins
  [1964] IR 374 .... 7.08, 7.09, 7.23, 8.08, 8.14
Attorney General (McLoughlin) v. Rhatigan (1966) 100 ILTR 37 ...... 2.15
Attorney General (Neagle) v. Crosbie, unreported, High Court, 6
  February 1975 .... 1.11
Attorney General (O'Gara) v. Callanan (1958) 52 ILTR 74 .... 8.11
Attorney General (Ruddy) v. Kenny (1960) 94 ILTR 185 .... 2.04, 2.06

Barker v. Wingo (1972) 407 US 514 .... 7.24
Boxer v. Snelling [1972] RTR 472 .... 2.12
Butler v. Mahon, unreported, High Court, 19 February 1988 ..... 8.15, 9.12
Butler v. Ruane, unreported, High Court, 21 July 1988 .... 8.09

Carpenter v. Kirby [1990] ILRM 764 .... 8.12
Christie v. Leachinsky [1947] AC 573 .... 3.14
Clune v. Director of Public Prosecutions [1981] ILRM 17 .... 8.04
Conroy v. Attorney General [1965] IR 411 .... 1.22, 6.05
Coughlan v. Patwell [1993] 1 IR 31 .... 7.03, 9.14
Cowzer v. Kirby, unreported, High Court, 11 February 1991 .... 8.04

Dawson v. Hamill [1989] IR 275; [1990] ILRM 257 .... 8.03
Dawson v. Hamill (No. 2) [1991] 1 IR 213 .... 9.14
Devereaux v. Kotsonouris [1992] ILRM 140 .... 9.15
Dillane v. Ireland [1980] ILRM 167 .... 8.16
Dineen v. Delap [1994] 2 IR 228 .... 8.03, 9.14

Director of Public Prosecutions v. Bouchier Hayes, unreported,
High Court, 19 December 1992............................ 7.24
Director of Public Prosecutions v. Brady [1991] 1 IR 337 .... 3.06, 3.07
Director of Public Prosecutions v. Breheny, unreported,
Supreme Court, 2 March 1993 .... 2.14
Director of Public Prosecutions v. Burnby, unreported, High Court,
24 July 1989... 7.24
Director of Public Prosecutions v. Byrne, unreported, Supreme Court,
21 March 1984... 4.12
Director of Public Prosecutions v. Byrne, 'Meath Chronicle',
1 June 1991 .... 4.03
Director of Public Prosecutions v. Byrne [1994] 2 IR 236 .... 7.24
Director of Public Prosecutions v. Carlton [1993] 1 IR 81............ 7.24
Director of Public Prosecutions v. Clein [1983] ILRM 76 .... 7.02
Director of Public Prosecutions v. Clinton [1984] ILRM 127.......... 4.04
Director of Public Prosecutions v. Closkey, unreported, High Court,
6 February 1984... 3.18
Director of Public Prosecutions v. Collins
[1981] ILRM 447 .... 4.10, 4.18, 5.04, 5.06, 5.09
Director of Public Prosecutions v. Connors [1992] 2 IR 125 .... 4.20
Director of Public Prosecutions v. Corbett (No. 1) [1991] 2 IR 1 ... 7.24, 8.07
Director of Public Prosecutions v. Corbett (No. 2)
[1992] ILRM 674 .... 7.24, 8.07
Director of Public Prosecutions v. Corrigan, unreported, High Court,
21 July 1980.. 4.18
Director of Public Prosecutions v. Corrigan [1986] IR 290; [1987]
ILRM 575 .... 3.19
Director of Public Prosecutions v. Cowman [1993] 1 IR 335 .... 3.03
Director of Public Prosecutions v. Cullen, unreported, High Court,
2 July 1984.. 5.07
Director of Public Prosecutions v. Daly, unreported, High Court,
3 March 1986... 3.15, 3.16
Director of Public Prosecutions v. Donoghue [1986] IR 188; [1987]
ILRM 129.. 3.02, 3.08, 3.11
Director of Public Prosecutions v. Doyle [1994] 2 IR 286; [1994] 1
ILRM 529 .... 5.08, 8.04
Director of Public Prosecutions v. Fahy (1987) 5 ILT (NS) 270......... 8.09
Director of Public Prosecutions v. Fanagan, unreported, High Court,
18 December 1991....................................... 3.02
Director of Public Prosecutions v. Flahive [1988] ILRM 133.......... 5.07
Director of Public Prosecutions v. Forbes [1994] 2 IR 542; [1993]
ILRM 817 .... 3.20
Director of Public Prosecutions v. Fountain [1988] RTR 385.......... 4.07
Director of Public Prosecutions v. Gaffney [1987] IR 173 .... 3.17, 3.18
Director of Public Prosecutions v. Gaughran [1993] 3 IR 598 .... 3.05
Director of Public Prosecutions v. Gill [1980] IR 263.... 7.12, 7.20, 7.24, 8.13
Director of Public Prosecutions v. Gilmore [1981] ILRM 102 ..... 3.08, 3.11

Table of Cases xiii

Director of Public Prosecutions v. Gray, unreported, High Court,
8 May 1987 .... 3.11
Director of Public Prosecutions v. Hand [1994] 1 IR 577 .... 4.05
Director of Public Prosecutions v. Haughey, unreported,
District Court, 7 September 1990 .... 5.11
Director of Public Prosecutions v. Hussey, unreported, High Court,
20 October 1987 .... 7.11
Director of Public Prosecutions v. Joyce [1985] ILRM 206 .... 3.02, 3.06
Director of Public Prosecutions v. Kemmy [1980] IR 160 ..... 3.02, 4.13, 8.03
Director of Public Prosecutions v. Kenny [1992] 2 IR 141............ 2.05
Director of Public Prosecutions v. Lynch [1991] 1 IR 43.............. 3.12
Director of Public Prosecutions v. McCreesh
[1992] 2 IR 239............................... 3.14, 3.19, 3.21
Director of Public Prosecutions v. McGarrigle, unreported,
Supreme Court, 22 June 1987 .... 4.05
Director of Public Prosecutions v. McGuoy, unreported, High Court,
25 July 1983.. 4.20
Director of Public Prosecutions v. McKillen [1991] 2 IR 508.......... 7.20
Director of Public Prosecutions v. McPartland [1983] ILRM 411 .... 5.07
Director of Public Prosecutions v. Maguire, unreported,
High Court, 29 April 1994 .... 7.11, 7.17
Director of Public Prosecutions v. Molloy [1994] 1 IR 583;
[1993] ILRM 573 .... 2.15, 2.16
Director of Public Prosecutions v. Mooney [1992] 1 IR 548;
[1993] ILRM 214 .... 3.14
Director of Public Prosecutions v. Nolan [1990] 2 IR 526;
[1989] ILRM 39 .... 7.17
Director of Public Prosecutions v. O'Connor [1985] ILRM 333 .... 3.13
Director of Public Prosecutions v. O'Donoghue [1991] 1 IR 448 .... 5.11
Director of Public Prosecutions v. O'Neill, unreported,
Supreme Court, 30 July 1984 .... 4.11, 5.06
Director of Public Prosecutions v. Ó Súilleabháin, unreported,
High Court, 5 May 1992 .... 3.13
Director of Public Prosecutions v. Roche and Kelly [1990] 2 IR 526;
[1989] ILRM 39 .... 7.17
Director of Public Prosecutions v. Sheehy [1987] ILRM 138 .... 3.22
Director of Public Prosecutions v. Sheeran [1986] ILRM 579 ..... 7.12, 7.20
Director of Public Prosecutions v. Shields, unreported, High Court,
4 December 1987 .... 7.17
Director of Public Prosecutions v. Smyth [1987] ILRM 570 .... 5.03
Director of Public Prosecutions v. Spaight, unreported, High Court,
27 November 1981 .... 4.18
Director of Public Prosecutions v. Spratt, unreported, High Court,
8 February 1995 .... 4.01
Director of Public Prosecutions v. Tuttle, unreported, High Court,
23 March 1987 .... 5.07
Director of Public Prosecutions v. Walsh [1985] ILRM 243........... 4.20

Director of Public Prosecutions v. Watkins [1989] 2 WLR 966;
   [1989] 1 All ER 1126; [1989] RTR 324. . . . . 2.19
Director of Public Prosecutions v. Winston, unreported, High Court,
   25 May 1992. . . . . 8.06
Director of Public Prosecutions (Coughlan) v. Swan [1994]
   1 ILRM 314. . . . . 4.06
Director of Public Prosecutions (Nagle) v. Flynn [1987] IR 534;
   [1989] ILRM 65 . . . . 7.11, 7.23, 9.03
Director of Public Prosecutions (Stratford) v. Fagan
   [1994] 2 ILRM 349. . . . . 3.03, 3.04
Donnelly v. Timber Factors Ltd [1991] 1 IR 553. . . . . 8.03
Duff v. Mangan [1994] 1 ILRM 91 . . . . 7.11, 9.15
Dunne v. Clinton [1930] IR 366 . . . . 3.16

Edkins v. Knowles [1973] RTR 257. . . . . 2.10
Emergency Powers Bill, 1976, In re [1977] IR 159 . . . . 4.02

Flynn v. Ruane [1989] ILRM 690 . . . . 8.09
Friel v. McMenamin [1990] 2 IR 210; [1990] ILRM 761. . . . . 8.02

G v. Director of Public Prosecutions [1994] 1 IR 374. . . . . 9.14
Gallagher v. O'Hanlon, unreported, High Court, 10 July 1975. . . . . 4.07
Gill v. Connellan [1987] IR 541; [1988] ILRM 448. . . . . 8.03
Grennan v. Kirby [1994] 2 ILRM 199 . . . . 8.09

Hanratty v. Kirby, unreported, High Court, 22 July 1993 . . . . 4.21
Heffron v. Hughes [1949] Ir Jur Rep 58. . . . . 6.04
Hegarty v. Fitzpatrick [1990] 2 IR 377. . . . . 8.02
Hobbs v. Hurley, unreported, High Court, 10 June 1980. . 3.11, 4.17, 4.18, 5.05

Irish Insurance Commissioners v. Trench (1913) 47 ILTR 115 . . . . 7.09

Joyce v. Circuit Court Judge for the Western Circuit [1987]
   ILRM 316 . . . . 6.05, 7.07

Keating v. The Governor of Mountjoy Prison [1991] 1 IR 61; [1990]
   ILRM 850 . . . . 4.03

Lawrence v. Howlett [1952] 2 All ER 74. . . . . 2.14
Leach v. Evans [1952] 2 All ER 264. . . . . 2.19
Le Gear v. Mangan, unreported, High Court, 16 December 1994. . . . . . 7.18
Lennon v. Clifford [1992] 1 IR 382; [1993] ILRM 77. . . . . 9.10, 9.11

McCarrick v. Leavy [1964] IR 225; (1965) 99 ILTR 163. . . . . 2.09
McCormack v. Carroll (1911) 45 ILTR 7 . . . . 7.01
McFadden, Ex parte [1888] Judgments of the Superior Courts (Irl)
   168 . . . . 9.03

Table of Cases

McGirl v. McArdle [1989] IR 596; [1989] ILRM 495 .... 7.02
McNally v. Martin, unreported, High Court, 14 January 1994 .... 8.03
Maguire v. Shelly [1992] 1 IR 482 .... 7.22
Maher v. Attorney General [1973] IR 140 .... 1.10
Maher v. Carroll, unreported, High Court, 8 August 1986 .... 7.24
Minister for Agriculture v. Norgro Ltd [1980] IR 155 .... 7.10
Minister for Justice v. Wang Zhu Jie [1993] 1 IR 426;
   [1991] ILRM 823 .... 9.08
Montgomery v. Loney [1959] NI 171 .... 2.16
Morris v. Long [1955-6] Ir Jur Rep 13 .... 8.11
Mulligan v. Tarpey, unreported, High Court, 15 July 1974 .... 1.11

O'Broin v. Ruane [1989] IR 214 .... 8.03
O'Connor v. Bannon, unreported, High Court, 15 December 1980 ...... 5.11
O'Mahony v. Melia [1989] IR 335; [1990] ILRM 14 .... 7.22

Pearlman v. Harrow School [1979] QB 56 .... 9.11
People (Attorney General) v. Poyning [1972] IR 402 .... 6.05
People (DPP) v. Conroy [1986] IR 460; [1988] ILRM 4 .... 4.02
People (DPP) v. Farrell [1978] IR 13 .... 2.09, 4.02
People (DPP) v. Greeley [1985] ILRM 320 .... 3.02, 3.10, 3.22
People (DPP) v. Healy [1990] 2 IR 73; [1990] ILRM 313 .... 4.02
People (DPP) v. Kehoe [1985] IR 444; [1986] ILRM 690 .... 3.23
People (DPP) v. McGinley Judgments of the Court of Criminal
   Appeal 1984-1989, p. 233 .... 3.16
People (DPP) v. Madden [1977] IR 336 .... 4.02
People (DPP) v. Pringle (1981) 2 Frewen 57 .... 4.02
People (DPP) v. Roddy [1977] IR 177 .... 7.01
People (DPP) v. Shaw [1982] IR 1 .... 3.22, 3.23, 4.02
People (DPP) v. Walsh [1980] IR 294 .... 3.14
Power v. Kirby, unreported, High Court, 23 April 1986 .... 7.02

R. v. John [1974] 1 WLR 624; [1974] 2 All ER 561; [1974] RTR 332 .... 4.07
R. v. Knightley [1971] 1 WLR 1073; [1971] 2 All ER 1041;
   [1971] RTR 409 .... 4.07
R. v. McDonagh [1974] RTR 372 .... 2.10
R. v. Padbury (1879) 5 QBD 126 .... 9.04
R. v. Paul [1952] NI 61 .... 2.14
R. v. Tashin [1970] RTR 88 .... 2.14
R. v. Tomlinson (1872) LR 8 QB 12 .... 9.04
R (Buck) v. Londonderry JJ [1952] NI 1 .... 8.15
R (Drohan) v. Waterford JJ [1900] 2 IR 307 .... 9.06
R (Martin) v. Mahony [1910] 2 IR 695 .... 9.10, 9.13
Rainey v. Delap [1988] IR 470; [1988] ILRM 620 .... 7.06
Rowland v. Thorpe [1970] 3 All ER 195; [1970] RTR 406 .... 4.07

Singh v. Ruane [1989] IR 610 .... 8.03, 9.14

Sports Arena Ltd v. O'Reilly [1987] IR 185 .... 9.06
State (Abenglen Properties Ltd) v. Dublin Corporation [1984] IR 381;
    [1982] ILRM 590 .... 9.15
State (Aherne) v. The Governor of Limerick Prison [1982] IR 188;
    [1983] ILRM 17 .... 9.03
State (Attorney General) v. Connolly [1948] IR 176 .... 9.03, 9.05
State (Attorney General) v. Mangan [1961] Ir Jur Rep 17 .... 8.09
State (Attorney General) v. Roe [1951] IR 172 .... 7.14, 8.01
State (Barr) v. McCay, unreported, High Court, 19 May 1980 .... 7.10
State (Byrne) v. Plunkett, unreported, High Court, 1 July 1985 .... 7.11
State (Caddle) v. McCarthy [1957] IR 359 .... 9.11
State (Clarke) v. Roche [1986] IR 619;
    [1987] ILRM 309 .... 7.05, 7.07, 7.11, 7.15, 7.16, 8.11, 8.12
State (Collins) v. Ruane [1984] IR 105; [1985] ILRM 349 .... 7.01
State (Collins) v. Kelleher [1983] IR 388 .... 2.02
State (Cronin) v. The Circuit Court Judge of the Western Circuit
    [1937] IR 34 .... 7.01
State (Cuddy) v. Mangan [1988] ILRM 720 .... 7.24
State (Cunningham) v. Ó Floinn [1960] IR 198 .... 8.14, 9.12
State (Davidson) v. Farrell [1960] IR 438 .... 9.11
State (de Burca) v. Ó hUadhaigh [1976] IR 85 .... 9.11
State (Delaney) v. Magee [1983] ILRM 45 .... 6.02
State (DPP) v. Roe [1985] IR 307 .... 8.16
State (Duggan) v. Evans (1978) 112 ILTR 61 .... 8.07
State (Gartlan) v. O'Donnell [1986] ILRM 588 .... 7.20
State (Healy) v. Donoghue [1976] IR 325 .... 8.02, 9.11, 9.13
State (Higgins) v. Reid [1983] ILRM 310 .... 5.08
State (Hoey) v. Garvey [1978] IR 1 .... 3.23
State (Kiernan) v. de Burca [1963] IR 348; (1965) 99 ILTR 14 .... 9.11
State (Llewellyn) v. Ua Donnchadha [1973] IR 151 .... 8.09
State (Lynch) v. Ballagh [1986] IR 203; (1987) ILRM 65 ...... 7.07, 7.22, 7.23
State (McCann) v. Wine [1981] IR 134 .... 8.01
State (McCarthy) v. O'Donnell [1945] IR 126 .... 9.05
State (McLoughlin) v. Shannon [1948] IR 439 .... 9.04, 9.05
State (Murray) v. Clifford, unreported, High Court, 4 February 1980 .... 3.09
State (O'Connell) v. Fawsitt [1986] IR 362; [1986] ILRM 639 .... 7.24
State (O'Connor) v. Larkin [1968] IR 255 .... 8.03
State (O'Leary) v. Neilan [1984] ILRM 35 .... 7.14
State (O'Regan) v. Plunkett [1984] ILRM 347 .... 4.19, 4.20, 4.21
State (O'Reilly) v. Windle, unreported, High Court,
    4 November 1986 .... 8.03
State (Prendergast) v. Porter [1961] Ir Jur Rep 14 .... 2.11
State (Quinn) v. Connellan, unreported, High Court, 9 July 1984 .... 4.10
State (Reilly) v. The Circuit Court Judge of the Midland Circuit
    [1936] IR 372; (1936) 70 ILTR 105 .... 9.11
State (Roche) v. Delap [1980] IR 170 .... 9.15
State (Sugg) v. O'Sullivan, unreported, High Court, 23 June 1980 .. 8.14, 8.15

Table of Cases

State (Taylor) v. The Circuit Court Judge for the County of Wicklow
  [1951] IR 311 .... 2.01, 2.09
State (Turley) v. Ó Floinn [1968] IR 245 .... 9.06, 9.08
State (Walsh) v. Maguire [1979] IR 372 .... 3.23
State (Walshe) v. Murphy [1981] IR 275 .... 4.19, 4.20, 4.21
State (White) v. Martin (1977) 111 ILTR 21 .... 9.04
Sullivan v. Robinson [1954] IR 161; (1954) 88 ILTR 169 .... 2.04
Sweeney v. Brophy [1993] 2 IR 202 .... 8.03, 9.14

Treacy v. Young, unreported, Supreme Court, 13 July 1983 .... 5.01

Verdon v. Downes, unreported, Supreme Court, 29 July 1976 ..... 1.11, 8.09

Walker v. Rountree [1963] NI 23 .... 2.19
Walsh v. Ó Buachalla [1991] 1 IR 56 .... 4.02, 4.03
Williams v. Osborne [1975] RTR 181 .... 2.19

Table of Statutes

Civil Bill Courts (Ireland) Act 1864
    s. 49 .... 9.04
County Officers and Courts (Ireland) Act 1877
    s. 72 .... 9.04
    s. 76 .... 9.04
Court Officers Act 1926
    s. 48 .... 7.05
Courts Act 1991
    s. 22 .... 7.18
Courts of Justice Act 1924
    s. 91 .... 7.06
Courts of Justice Act 1928
    s. 18(1) 9.01
    s. 18(3) 9.01, 9.05
Courts of Justice Act 1936
    s. 58 .... 9.01
Courts of Justice Act 1953
    s. 27(3) 8.09
    s. 33 .... 9.01
Courts (No. 2) Act 1986
    s. 2 .... 6.01
Courts (No. 3) Act 1986
    s. 1(1) 7.16
    s. 1(2) 7.16
    s. 1(3) 7.16
    s. 1(4) 7.16, 7.17
    s. 1(7) (a) 7.16, 7.17, 7.20
Courts (Supplemental Provisions) Act 1961
    s. 50 .... 9.03
    s. 51(1) 9.06
    s. 51(2) 9.06
    s. 51(3) 9.06
    s. 52 .... 9.07
    s. 52(2) 9.08
Criminal Justice Act 1951
    s. 15(2) 7.22

Criminal Justice Act 1951 (*contd.*)
    s. 15(3) 7.22
    s. 15(4) 7.22
    s. 15(5) 7.22
    s. 15(6) 7.22
    s. 23 .... 9.16
    s. 26 .... 8.11
Criminal Justice Act 1984
    s. 7(3) 4.01
    s. 7(4) 4.01
    s. 26 .... 7.22
Criminal Justice (Administration) Act 1924
    s. 9(2) 7.01
Criminal Procedure Act 1967
    s. 31(1) 7.22
Interpretation Act 1937
    s. 11(h) 7.10
Licensing Act 1872
    s. 12 .... 1.01
Medical Practitioners Act 1978
    s. 26 .... 5.10
Motor Car Act 1903
    s. 1 .... 1.01
Offences against the State Act 1939
    s. 30 .... 3.23, 4.02
Petty Sessions (Ireland) Act 1851
    s. 10 .... 7.04, 7.07, 7.09, 7.17
    s. 10(4) 7.12
    s. 11 .... 7.04
    s. 20 .... 8.01
    s. 20(4) 8.02
    s. 21 .... 8.11
    s. 24(6) 9.04
Probation of Offenders Act 1907
    s. 1(1) 6.09, 6.11
Prosecution of Offences Act 1974
    s. 3(1) 7.01, 9.06
Road Traffic Act 1933
    s. 30 .... 1.01, 6.04
Road Traffic Act 1961
    s. 3(1) 2.10, 2.12, 2.15
    s. 3(2) 2.13
    s. 4(2) 3.24
    s. 26(1) 6.05, 6.09, 6.11
    s. 26(4) 6.08
    s. 26(4)(a) 6.09, 6.11
    s. 26(4)(b) 6.09

Road Traffic Act 1961 (*contd.*)

s. 26(5)	6.08
s. 26(6)	6.09, 6.11
s. 26(8)	6.09, 6.11
s. 27(1)(a)	6.05
s. 27(1)(b)	6.05
s. 28(1)	6.05
s. 28(2)	6.05
s. 29(1)(a)	6.08
s. 29(1A)(a)	6.08
s. 29(1A)(b)	6.08
s. 29(1)(b)	6.08
s. 29(2)	6.08
s. 29(3)	6.08
s. 29(5)	6.08
s. 29(6)	6.08
s. 30(1)	6.06
s. 30(3)(a)	6.06
s. 30(3)(c)	6.07, 9.02
s. 30(3)(d)	6.06
s. 30(3)(e)	6.06
s. 30(4)	6.07
s. 30(5)	6.07
s. 36(3)(a)	6.09, 6.11
s. 49	1.03, 1.04, 1.05, 1.07, 1.10, 1.12, 1.19, 1.22, 2.01, 2.02, 2.17, 2.20, 3.01, 3.05, 3.07, 3.10, 3.11, 3.16, 3.19, 3.20, 3.21, 4.05, 4.06, 4.07, 4.17, 4.22, 5.10, 5.11, 6.02, 6.09, 6.11, 8.09, 8.16
s 49(1)	1.02, 2.03, 2.05, 2.06, 2.20, 3.08
s. 49(1)(a)	2.01, 2.02, 2.03
s. 49(1)(b)	2.03
s. 49(2)	2.01, 2.02, 2.03, 2.07, 3.07, 3.08, 3.10, 5.01, 5.02
s. 49(3)	2.01, 2.02, 2.03, 2.07, 3.08, 3.10, 5.01, 5.02
s. 49(4)	2.01, 3.10, 4.23
s. 49(6)(a)	6.09
s. 49(6)(b)	2.02
s. 49(7)	6.09
s. 49(8)	2.21, 3.01, 3.10, 3.21, 3.22, 4.04
s. 50	1.10, 2.02, 2.17, 2.18, 2.20, 3.01, 3.05, 3.10, 3.16, 3.21, 4.05, 4.07, 4.22, 5.10, 5.11, 6.09, 6.11, 8.16
s. 50(1)	2.18, 2.20
s. 50(1)(a)	2.17
s. 50(2)	2.17
s. 50(3)	2.17
s. 50(4)	2.17, 4.23
s. 50(6)(a)	6.09
s. 50(6)(b)	2.18

Road Traffic Act 1961 (contd.)
 s. 50(7) 6.09
 s. 50(8) 2.18
 s. 50(10) 2.21, 3.01, 3.10, 3.21, 3.22, 4.04
 s. 53 .... 8.01
 s. 53(6) 3.22, 4.04
 s. 106(3A) 3.22, 4.04
 s. 107 .... 2.09
 s. 109(1) 3.03, 3.16
 s. 110 .... 3.24
 s. 112(6) 3.22, 4.04
 s. 124 .... 9.16

Road Traffic Act 1968
 s. 6 .... 3.16
 s. 19 .... 6.08
 s. 20 .... 6.06, 6.07, 9.02
 s. 28 .... 1.06
 s. 29 .... 1.05
 s. 30 .... 4.07

Road Traffic Act 1994
 s. 3(1) 5.09
 s. 9(1) 5.10, 5.11
 s. 10 .... 2.01, 2.02, 2.03, 2.21, 3.01, 3.10, 6.09
 s. 11 .... 2.17, 2.18, 2.21, 3.01, 3.10, 6.09
 s. 12 .... 3.05, 3.06, 3.07, 3.10, 3.16, 6.10
 s. 12(1) 3.01
 s. 12(1)(a) 3.05
 s. 12(1)(b) 3.05, 3.15, 3.16
 s. 12(1)(c) 3.05, 3.16
 s. 12(2) 3.01, 3.05, 6.10
 s. 12(3) 3.01, 3.05, 3.10, 3.22, 4.04
 s. 12(4) 3.05, 3.09
 s. 13 .... 3.10, 3.22, 4.04, 4.05, 4.07, 5.10,
  .... 5.11, 6.08, 6.09, 6.11, 8.16
 s. 13(1) 3.01, 4.22, 5.10
 s. 13(1)(a) 4.04
 s. 13(1)(b) 4.04, 4.05, 4.06
 s. 13(2) 3.01, 4.22, 6.11
 s. 13(3) 3.01, 4.04, 4.06, 6.11
 s. 13(4) 4.22
 s. 13(5) 6.11
 s. 14 .... 2.21, 5.10, 6.08, 6.09, 6.11, 8.16
 s. 14(1) 2.21
 s. 14(2) 2.21, 6.11
 s. 14(3) 2.21
 s. 14(4) 2.22, 5.10
 s. 14(5) 2.22, 6.11

Road Traffic Act 1994 (*contd.*)

s. 14(6)	6.11
s. 15	4.09, 5.10, 6.08, 6.09, 6.11, 8.16
s. 15(1)	4.08, 5.10
s. 15(2)	4.09, 6.11
s. 15(3)	4.09
s. 15(4)	6.11
s. 16	4.14, 4.15
s. 16(1)	4.14
s. 16(2)	4.15
s. 16(3)(a)	4.15
s. 16(3)(b)	4.15
s. 17	4.24, 6.12
s. 17(1)	4.22
s. 17(2)	4.23
s. 17(3)	4.23
s. 17(3)(a)	4.24
s. 17(4)	4.23, 6.12
s. 17(5)	4.24
s. 18	2.22
s. 18(1)	3.01, 4.10
s. 18(2)	3.01, 4.12
s. 18(3)	3.01, 4.12
s. 18(4)	3.02, 4.12
s. 19	2.22, 5.05
s. 19(1)	3.01, 4.16
s. 19(2)	4.16
s. 19(3)	3.01, 4.16, 4.17
s. 19(4)	4.16
s. 20	2.20, 6.13
s. 20(1)	2.20
s. 20(2)	2.20
s. 20(3)	2.20
s. 20(3)(a)	6.13
s. 20(3)(b)	6.13
s. 20(4)	2.20
s. 21	4.18
s. 21(1)	4.24
s. 21(2)	3.01, 5.01
s. 21(3)	3.01, 3.02, 4.16, 5.02, 5.04, 5.06
s. 21(4)	3.02, 5.10
s. 22(1)	8.16
s. 23(1)	4.22
s. 23(2)	4.07, 4.09
s. 23(3)	4.07
s. 24	2.03, 2.18
s. 26	6.05, 6.08, 6.09, 6.11

Road Traffic Act 1994 (*contd.*)
    s. 27 .... 6.08
    s. 39(3) 4.08
    s. 39(4) 4.08
    s. 41 .... 3.24
    s. 49(1)(a)(iv) 2.15
    s. 49(1)(c) 6.05
    s. 49(1)(k) 3.24
    s. 49(1)(l) 6.09, 6.11
Road Traffic Act 1995
    s. 2 .... 6.09, 6.11
    s. 3 .... 6.09
Road Traffic (Amendment) Act 1978
    s. 13 .... 3.10, 4.03, 4.05, 6.09, 6.11
    s. 13(3) 8.15
    s. 14 .... 4.05, 6.09, 6.11
    s. 17 .... 6.09, 6.11
    s. 22 .... 5.05
    s. 22(3) 4.17
    s. 23 .... 4.18
    s. 23(2) 5.04, 5.06
Summary Jurisdiction Act 1857
    s. 2 .... 9.06
    s. 4 .... 9.06
    s. 5 .... 9.06
    s. 6 .... 9.06
    s. 14 .... 9.06

An Historical Introduction

1.01 The beginning Section 12 of the Licensing Act 1872 (which is still in force) provides that: 'Every person . . . who is drunk while in charge on any highway or other public place of any carriage, horse, cattle or steam engine . . . may be apprehended, and shall be liable to a penalty not exceeding forty shillings, or in the discretion of the court to imprisonment with or without hard labour for any term not exceeding one month.' This remained the sole statutory prohibition in respect of drinking and driving (although the Motor Car Act 1903, section 1, created an offence of reckless driving) until the Road Traffic Act 1933. Section 30 of the 1933 Act made it an offence to drive or attempt to drive a mechanically propelled vehicle in a public place while drunk and provided that a person was to be deemed drunk if he was incapable of exercising effective control of the vehicle while in motion by reason of the consumption of intoxicating liquor or drugs. Conviction for a first offence under section 30 rendered the person liable to a fine not exceeding £50 and to a term of imprisonment not exceeding three months; a subsequent offence carried a maximum fine of £100 and a term of imprisonment not exceeding six months. The 1933 Act introduced the consequential disqualification order on a conviction for drunken driving; in other words, on conviction the court was bound, in addition to any other punishment, to disqualify the person from holding a driving licence for not less than 12 months in the case of a first offence and not less than three years in the case of any subsequent offence.

1.02 The Road Traffic Act 1961 Section 49(1) of the 1961 Act provided that: 'A person shall not drive or attempt to drive a mechanically propelled vehicle in a public place while he is under the influence of intoxicating liquor or a drug to such an extent as to be incapable of having proper control of the vehicle.' On conviction the person was liable to imprisonment for a term not exceeding six months or to a fine not exceeding £100 or to both the imprisonment and fine. As under the 1933 Act, conviction resulted in a mandatory disqualification for a period of not less than one year in the case of a first offence and not less than three years in the case of a subsequent offence.

1.03 Under the 1933 Act the offence was committed where the person drove 'while he is drunk'. This not surprisingly led judges to take the view that the offence was not committed unless it was shown that the defendant was drunk in the sense that he was overcome by liquor. Consequently, there was a shift in the emphasis under section 49: the word 'drunk' does not appear; instead the essence of the offence is driving while under the influence to such an extent as to be incapable of having proper control. Section 49 also made alterations in relation to the penalties. Imprisonment was now the first penalty and the fine was the alternative, and the term of imprisonment in the case of a first offence was increased to six months. In addition, the court was precluded from applying the Probation of Offenders Act 1907 to an offence under the section.

1.04 The Davitt Commission Report Notwithstanding the changes, it was felt the 1961 Act was ineffective in controlling drinking and driving, largely because of the absence of a fixed standard for the purpose of determining incapacity to drive a motor vehicle. In 1961 a commission was established under the chairmanship of the then President of the High Court, Cahir Davitt, and its terms of reference required it to investigate the feasibility of fixing a standard by reference to the alcohol content of the blood or by any other test so as to establish drunkenness for the purpose of the offence of drunken driving. In its report the commission concluded[1] that 'A sufficiently high concentration of alcohol in the brain will render a person unfit to drive. The concentration of alcohol in the blood (described as the "blood-alcohol level") is a reliable measure of the concentration of alcohol in the brain; and it can be ascertained with reasonable accuracy by scientific methods. A significant blood-alcohol level can be regarded, therefore, as satisfactory evidence of serious worsening of a person's capacity to drive.' The commission recommended that section 49 of the 1961 Act be amended so as to prohibit a person from driving or attempting to drive a mechanically propelled vehicle in a public place when he is unfit to do so by reason of the consumption of intoxicating liquor or drug to such an extent that his driving is likely to be a source of danger to the public or to himself. It further recommended that the person's blood-alcohol should be a factor in determining his fitness to drive and that proof that his blood-alcohol level exceeded 125 milligrammes at the material time

1 'Driving While Under the Influence of Drink or a Drug', Pr. 7165, pp. 50-51.

or within three hours thereafter should constitute prima facie evidence of unfitness.

1.05 The Road Traffic Act 1968 Following publication of the Davitt report it was announced that the Government accepted the main import of the report's recommendations, but wished to consider further whether a specified blood-alcohol level should be taken as conclusive proof of an offence or merely as prima facie proof as had been recommended by the commission. Ultimately a decision was taken in favour of making it an offence to drive when the blood-alcohol level exceeded a specified level. Hence section 29 of the 1968 Act amended section 49 of the 1961 Act by creating an alternative offence: a driver was now prohibited from driving or attempting to drive a mechanically propelled vehicle in a public place 'while there is present in his body a quantity of alcohol such that, within three hours after so driving or attempting to drive, the concentration of alcohol in his blood will exceed a concentration of 125 milligrammes of alcohol per 100 millilitres of blood'. The penalty applicable to the original offence under section 49 also applied to the new offence.

1.06 Having thus created a relatively technical offence, the 1968 Act inevitably contained the first complex provisions outlining a sequence of events which would lead to a conviction for the offence. Section 28 empowered a member of the Garda Síochána, when of the opinion that a person in charge of a mechanically propelled vehicle in a public place had consumed intoxicating liquor, to require him to provide a specimen of his breath by exhaling into an apparatus designed for the purpose of indicating the presence of alcohol in the breath. Failing this preliminary breath test (the 'breathalyser') was not of itself an offence; the test was designed as an indicator to the garda whether or not to take further action against the driver. But should the person refuse or fail to comply with the garda's requisition, that was an offence and rendered him liable to arrest.

1.07 After arrest for either drunken driving under section 49 or for refusal or failure to comply with a garda's requisition in relation to a breathalyser, the person was to be brought to a garda station. Once there it was provided that the member of the garda station then in charge might: (a) require the arrested person to provide a specimen of his breath by exhaling into an apparatus designed for showing the concentration of alcohol in the breath or blood or into a receptacle designed for preserving the specimen for subsequent analysis and/or (b) require him to permit a designated registered medical practitioner to take from him a specimen of his blood or, if he so opted, to provide for the registered medical practitioner a specimen of his urine. If an arrested person opted to give urine, but failed to do so, the member in charge could require him to permit a designated registered medical practitioner to take a specimen of his blood. A person who, following the appropriate requisition, refused or failed to permit the designed registered medical practitioner to take a specimen of his blood was guilty of an offence carrying the same penalties, including disqualification, as an offence under section 49.

1.08 The 1968 Act also provided for the establishment of a body referred to as the bureau (and later formally known as the Medical Bureau of Road Safety) whose functions included the receipt and analysis of specimens of blood and urine, the determination of the concentration of alcohol in those specimens, the provision of equipment for the taking or provision of specimens of blood and urine, and the issue of certificates. On receipt by the bureau of a specimen of blood or urine a part of the specimen had to be analysed and the concentration of alcohol in it determined. The result of the determination was set out in a certificate which was then issued to the member of the Garda Síochána in charge of the station from which the specimen had been forwarded. A statement containing the result of the determination was also issued to the person from whom the specimen had been obtained. The bureau's certificate was given a special evidential value: it was to be 'conclusive evidence' that, at the time the specimen was obtained, the concentration of the alcohol in the blood was the specified concentration of alcohol.

1.09 Elaborate safeguards for the protection of a suspected drunken driver were contained in the Act. A person whose blood or urine specimen had been analysed could, subject to certain conditions including payment of a fee, require the bureau to analyse portion of the remainder of his specimen and to determine the concentration of alcohol in it. He could also require that the analysis and determination be made in his presence or in the presence of a person nominated by him. The result of the second analysis was again set out in a certificate, and it was provided that if the concentration of alcohol specified in the second certificate was lower than that specified in the first certificate, the first certificate would be read as if the lower concentration had been specified in it. Furthermore, a person who gave a blood or urine specimen had to be given an opportunity of furnishing an additional specimen to a registered medical practitioner of his own choice; and if he so requested, he had to be supplied by the police doctor with an additional specimen of blood or portion of the specimen of urine.

1.10 The Road Traffic (Amendment) Act 1973 This Act attempted to ease somewhat the burden on the gardaí enforcing the drunken driving provisions of the 1968 Act. Thus under the 1968 Act the requirement that the arrested person brought to a garda station provide a specimen of his breath or furnish a blood or urine specimen had to be made by 'the member of the Garda Síochána then in charge there'. The 1973 Act altered the law so that henceforth an ordinary member of the Garda Síochána could make the requirement. It also created a presumption in a prosecution for an offence under section 49 (drunken driving) or 50 (drunk in charge) that a person who took a specimen of blood from an arrested person or for whom an arrested person provided a specimen of urine was a registered medical practitioner. But the evidential value of the certificate issued by the bureau was reduced by the 1973 Act: instead of being 'conclusive evidence' it would now be 'sufficient evidence until the contrary is shown'.[2]

1.11 Technical difficulties Notwithstanding the changes wrought by the 1973 Act, the machinery for dealing with drunken driving prosecutions in the 1968 Act became a victim of its own complexity. Under its provisions the Road Traffic Act 1968 (Part V) Regulations, 1969[3] prescribed forms for the certificate issued by the Medical Bureau of Road Safety and the certificate to be completed by the registered medical practitioner who obtained a blood or urine specimen and provided for procedural matters connected with taking blood and urine samples. In *Attorney General v. Hollingsworth*[4] the Supreme Court held that the regulations were not complied with where a blood specimen had been sent to the bureau in a tube which had been stopped with a screwed-on screw-top, because the regulations required that the tube be stopped with a stopper which would seal it. Following the decision in *Hollingsworth* amendments were made to the 1969 regulations by the Road Traffic Act 1968 (Part V) (Amendment) Regulations, 1973.[5] But in *Mulligan v. Tarpey*[6] it was held that the doctor's certificate, which proved compliance with certain requirements under the

---

2   This amendment was necessitated by the Supreme Court decision in *Maher v. Attorney General* [1973] IR 140 where it was held that rendering the bureau's certificate 'conclusive evidence' of the alcohol concentration, as the 1968 Act purported to do, infringed the judicial power of the District Court and was unconstitutional.
3   SI No. 196 of 1969.
4   (1973) 107 ILTR 77.
5   SI No. 138 of 1973.
6   Unreported judgment of the High Court (Ó Caoimh P) delivered 15 July 1974 which was followed in *Attorney General (Neagle) v. Crosbie*, unreported judgment of the High Court (Finlay P, as he then was) delivered 6 February 1975.

1969 regulations, did not prove compliance with those regulations as amended by the 1973 regulations. Finally in *Verdon v. Downes*[7] it was held that the bureau's certificate failed to show compliance with all the matters required to be proved in a drunken driving prosecution and that, until the certificate was amended[8] to include the matters omitted, the appropriate witness from the bureau would have to give oral evidence to prove them.

1.12 The Road Traffic (Amendment) Act 1978 The 1978 Act amended section 49 of the 1961 Act by inserting a wholly new section.[9] Under the new section 49 it was, first, an offence for a person to drive or attempt to drive a mechanically propelled vehicle in a public place while he was under the influence of an intoxicant to such an extent as to be incapable of having proper control of the vehicle. Secondly, it was an offence for a person to drive or attempt to drive a mechanically propelled vehicle in a public place while there was present in his body a quantity of alcohol such that, within three hours after so driving or attempting to drive, the concentration of alcohol in his blood exceeded a concentration of 100 milligrammes of alcohol per 100 millilitres of blood. Thirdly, it was an offence for a person so to drive or attempt to drive while there was present in his body a quantity of alcohol such that, within three hours, the concentration of alcohol in his urine exceeded a concentration of 135 milligrammes of alcohol per 100 millilitres of urine. Conviction for any of these offences rendered the person liable to a term of imprisonment not exceeding six months and/or a fine not exceeding £500; the court was required to make a consequential disqualification order, the minimum period of disqualification being one year in the case of a first offence and three years in the case of a second or subsequent offence; and the Probation of Offenders Act 1907 did not apply.

1.13 As in the case of the 1968 Act, the 1978 Act prescribed a sequence of events.[10] A garda was empowered to breathalyse a person in charge of a mechanically propelled vehicle in a public place if of the opinion that he had consumed intoxicating liquor. Failure or refusal to comply with this requirement was an offence and rendered the person liable to arrest. If of the opinion that a person was committing or had committed an offence

---

7   Unreported decision of the Supreme Court, judgment of Griffin J delivered 29 July 1976.
8   As it was by the Road Traffic Act 1968 (Part V) (Amendment) Regulations, 1976, SI No. 240 of 1976.
9   See the first edition of this book, pp. 25-28.
10 See the first edition of this book, pp. 39-62.

An Historical Introduction 7

under sections 49 or 50 (drunk in charge), a garda was empowered to arrest him. After the person had been brought to a garda station a garda might do either or both of the following: (a) require him to provide a specimen of his breath by exhaling into an apparatus for indicating the concentration of alcohol in breath or blood (in practice it appears this was never done except on an experimental basis); (b) require him either to permit a designated registered medical practitioner to take from him a specimen of his blood or, at his option, to provide for the designated registered medical practitioner a specimen of his urine. Refusal or failure to comply with the garda's requirement, or to comply with a requirement of a designated registered medical practitioner in relation to the taking or provision of a blood or urine specimen, was an offence.

1.14 After the specimen had been furnished the designated registered medical practitioner divided it into two parts, placed each part in a container which he sealed, and completed the prescribed form. A garda offered one of the sealed containers to the person together with a statement in writing that he might retain either of them. He was then bound, as soon as practicable, to cause the completed doctor's form together with one of the sealed containers, or both of them when the person had declined to retain one, to be forwarded to the Medical Bureau of Road Safety. The bureau was required, as soon as practicable after it had received a specimen, to analyse it and determine the concentration of alcohol. It then forwarded, as soon as practicable, a completed certificate in the prescribed form showing the result of the analysis to the garda station from which the specimen had been forwarded and a copy of the completed certificate to the person named on the doctor's form as the person from whom the specimen had been taken. The duly completed doctor's form and the bureau's certificate were sufficient evidence of the facts stated or certified in them until the contrary was shown.

1.15 The Road Traffic (Amendment) Act 1984 The purpose of this Act was to increase the penalties for road traffic offences. Under its provisions the maximum fine on conviction for a drunken driving offence under section 49 rose from £500 to £1,000. No alteration was made in relation to the custodial penalty (imprisonment for a term not exceeding six months) or the disqualification requirement.

1.16 The Road Traffic Act 1994 The 1994 Act was designed to restate and strengthen the law relating to drunken driving. In addition, it provided new measures to improve enforcement of the Road Traffic Acts; for example, a person driving a mechanically propelled vehicle in a public place must now produce a current driver's licence on demand by a garda, whereas under the 1961 Act he was allowed 10 days within which to produce it. The 1994 Act also introduced new arrangements for making traffic regulations and devolved certain functions in relation to speed limits, parking controls and traffic management to local authorities.

1.17 Part III of the 1994 Act deals with drunken driving offences and was brought into force on 2 December 1994.[11] The principal new features in the law are as follows. The maximum permissible alcohol level for drivers has been reduced to 80 (from 100) milligrammes of alcohol per 100 millilitres of blood and to 107 (from 135) milligrammes of alcohol per 100 millilitres of urine. There is now a maximum permissible breath alcohol level: 35 microgrammes of alcohol per 100 millilitres of breath. Furthermore, the Minister for the Environment is empowered by making regulations to vary these limits whether generally or in respect of a particular class of person.

1.18 The 1994 Act confers significant new powers on the gardaí. Doubts about the scope of the power of arrest have been addressed: a garda is now expressly empowered for the purpose of arresting a person for drunken driving to 'enter without warrant (if need be by use of reasonable force) any place (including the curtilage of a dwelling but not including a dwelling) where the person is or where the member, with reasonable cause, suspects him to be'. If a driver is injured or claims to have been injured and is admitted to hospital, a garda is empowered to require him to furnish a blood or urine specimen to a designated doctor; it is a defence to refusing or failing to comply with a garda's requirement in such circumstances if the driver has come under the care of a doctor and he, on medical grounds, refuses to permit the furnishing of the specimen; and for the purpose of obtaining the specimen the garda and designated doctor are empowered to enter the hospital where the person is. Finally, a person arrested for drunken driving may be detained in custody for a period not exceeding six hours from the time of arrest if the garda in charge of the station is of the opinion that he is under the influence of an intoxicant to such an extent as to be a threat to the safety of himself or others; but generally he must be released upon the attendance at the garda station of a relative or other person specified by him.

---

11 Road Traffic Act 1994 (Commencement) (No. 2) Order, 1994, SI No. 350 of 1994.

1.19 Under the 1994 Act the maximum monetary and custodial penalties on conviction for a drunken driving offence under section 49 remain unchanged (a fine not exceeding £1,000 and/or imprisonment for a term not exceeding six months), but the period of automatic disqualification was generally increased from one year to two years in the case of a first offence and from three years to four years in the case of a second or subsequent offence. Moreover, a person disqualified for an offence under section 49 usually remained disqualified until he produced a certificate of competency, in other words, until he passed a driving test.

1.20 The controversy surrounding the 1994 Act The introduction of the 1994 Act, with its reduced blood/alcohol limit and increased penalties, proved remarkably controversial. The principal objection was that the new legislation would be particularly hard felt in remote rural areas where the pub is a centre of social activity and where there is no adequate public transport or taxi services. As one TD graphically put it, the new Act would 'close down' rural Ireland. In response the Government indicated that it was not prepared to increase the legal limit, but the Minister for the Environment introduced proposals to grade the penalties for drunken driving offences which were enacted in the Road Traffic Act 1995.

1.21 The Road Traffic Act 1995 The 1995 Act abolished the requirement that a person disqualified for a drunken driving offence produce a certificate of competency to the appropriate licensing authority. It also reduced the period of disqualification at the lower levels of alcohol concentration in the blood, urine or breath. Lastly, the Act contained transitional provisions enabling a person convicted under subsections (2) or (3) of sections 49 and 50 for an offence committed on or after 2 December 1994, but before the passing of the 1995 Act, to apply to the court which disqualified him for a reduction in the period of disqualification and enabled the court to substitute a period of disqualification which would have been imposed if the offence had been committed after the passing of the 1995 Act.

1.22 The constitutionality of section 49: Conroy v. The Attorney General[12] Patrick Conroy was charged in the Dublin District Court with driving a mechanically propelled vehicle in a public place while under the influence of an intoxicating liquor or drug to such an extent as to be incapable of having proper control of the vehicle contrary to section 49 of

---

12 [1965] IR 411.

the Road Traffic Act 1961. He instituted proceedings in the High Court claiming (*inter alia*) a declaration that the provisions of the 1961 Act which enabled a person charged with an offence under section 49 to be tried by a court of summary jurisdiction were repugnant to the provisions of the Constitution. In support of his claim Mr Conroy relied on article 38 of the Constitution; section 2 of the article provides that 'Minor offences may be tried by courts of summary jurisdiction'; and section 5 provides that 'Save in the case of offences under section 2, section 3 (dealing with special courts established when the ordinary courts are inadequate to secure the effective administration of justice) and section 4 (dealing with military tribunals) of this Article no person shall be tried on any criminal charge without a jury.' The issue therefore was whether an offence under section 49 could be characterised as a 'minor offence' and so was triable in a summary manner in accordance with the Constitution. In the High Court Kenny J held that it was not. But on appeal to the Supreme Court it was held[13] that 'The primary consideration in determining whether an offence be a minor one or not is the punishment which it may attract.' Walsh J examined carefully the penalties for drunken driving, at that time imprisonment for six months or a fine of £100 or both. The argument was rejected that because a District Justice might under the District Court Rules order that, in default of payment of a fine of £100, the offender be committed to prison for six months, the effective maximum custodial penalty was imprisonment for 12 months. 'Imprisonment in default,' said Walsh J,[14] 'is not primarily a matter of punishment but is a method of distraining for the fine imposed and is a procedural matter rather than a substantive matter of punishment.' The court also rejected the argument that the consequential disqualification which follows on conviction under section 49 should be regarded not just as a punishment, but one so severe as to take the offence out of the category of a minor offence. Such a disqualification, it was held, is not in essence a punishment: 'it is essentially a finding of unfitness of the person concerned to hold a driving licence' and '(i)n so far as it may be classed as a punishment at all it is not a primary or direct punishment but rather an order which may, according to the circumstances of the particular individual concerned, assume, though remotely, a punitive character.'[15] Mr Conroy's claim to a declaration was, accordingly, refused.

13 *Per* Walsh J, delivering the judgment of the court, at p. 436 of the report; 'The moral quality of the act is a relevant though a secondary consideration': ibid.

14 At p. 437 of the report.
15 P. 441 of the report.

2

Drunken Driving, Drunk in Charge and Related Offences

INTRODUCTION

2.01 Section 49 of the Road Traffic Act 1961 as inserted by section 10 of the Road Traffic Act 1994 creates four[1] separate drunken driving offences. First, it is an offence for a person to drive or attempt to drive a mechanically propelled vehicle in a public place while he is under the influence of an intoxicant to such an extent as to be incapable of having proper control of the vehicle.[2] Secondly, it is an offence for a person to drive or attempt to drive a mechanically propelled vehicle in a public place while there is present in his body a quantity of alcohol such that, within three hours after so driving or attempting to drive, the concentration of alcohol in his blood exceeds a concentration of 80 milligrammes of alcohol per 100 millilitres of blood.[3] Thirdly, it is an offence for a person to drive or attempt to drive a mechanically propelled vehicle in a public place while there is present in his body a quantity of alcohol such that, within three hours after so driving or attempting to drive, the concentration of alcohol in his urine exceeds a concentration of 107 milligrammes of alcohol per 100 millilitres of urine.[4] Fourthly, it is an offence for a person to drive or attempt to drive a mechanically propelled vehicle in public place while there is present in his body a quantity of alcohol such that, within three hours after so driving or attempting to drive, the concentration of alcohol in his breath will exceed a concentration of 35 microgrammes of alcohol per 100 millilitres of breath.[5] The last of these offences (driving when the

---

1   Strictly speaking there are eight offences when one remembers that an attempt is a separate offence: *State (Taylor) v. The Circuit Court Judge for the County of Wicklow* [1951] IR 311.
2   Section 49(1)(a) of the 1961 Act as inserted by section 10 of the 1994 Act.
3   Section 49(2) of the 1961 Act as inserted by section 10 of the 1994 Act.
4   Section 49(3) of the 1961 Act as inserted by section 10 of the 1994 Act.
5   Section 49(4) of the 1961 Act as inserted by section 10 of the 1994 Act.

breath/alcohol level exceeds the prescribed limit) is a new offence created by the 1994 Act.

2.02 It has been held by the Supreme Court that a defendant may not be convicted of offences arising out of the same incident under both section 49(1)(a) (driving while under the influence of an intoxicant) and either section 49(2) or (3) (driving when the blood/alcohol or urine/alcohol level exceeds the prescribed limit).[6] However, a person charged with an offence under section 49 may be found guilty of an offence under section 50.[7]

DRIVING WHILE UNDER THE INFLUENCE OF AN INTOXICANT: SECTION 49(1)(a) OF THE 1961 ACT

2.03 Where this offence is alleged against a defendant the court has to determine whether, as a matter of fact, he drove while under the influence of an intoxicant to such an extent as to have been incapable of having proper control of the vehicle. This charge is frequently preferred where the defendant has failed to provide a blood or urine specimen for analysis with the result that it is not possible to bring a case under either section 49(2) or 49(3). Section 24 of the 1994 Act expressly provides that it is not a defence for a person charged under section 49(1) to show that an analysis has not been carried out or that he was not requested to provide a breath specimen. The elements of an offence under section 49(1)(a) may be summarised as follows:

1. There must be evidence that the defendant drove or attempted to drive.[8]

2. He must have driven or attempted to drive a mechanically propelled vehicle.[9]

3. The driving or attempt to drive must have taken place in a public place.[10]

4. The defendant must on the occasion have been under the influence of an intoxicant to such an extent as to have been unable to have proper control of the vehicle.[11]

---

6 *State (Collins) v. Kelleher* [1983] IR 388.
7 Section 49(6)(b) of the 1961 Act as inserted by section 10 of the 1994 Act.
8 See paras. 2.09-2.11 infra.
9 See paras. 2.12-2.14 infra.
10 See paras. 2.15-2.16 infra.
11 An 'intoxicant' includes alcohol and drugs and any combination of drugs or of drugs and alcohol: section 49(1)(b) of the 1961 Act as inserted by section 10 of the 1994 Act.

2.04 Evidence that the defendant was under the influence of an intoxicant It is this last requirement which, in practice, usually creates the greatest difficulty for the prosecution. As evidence that the defendant was under the influence of an intoxicant to the prohibited extent the prosecution may rely on a garda's testimony as to his observations in relation to the defendant's condition and his opinion derived from those observations.[12] It may also rely on the quality of the defendant's driving before he was apprehended. The prosecution's case will be greatly strengthened if a doctor is called to give evidence in relation to the defendant's condition and the evidence supports that of the garda. It is important to remember that the prosecution's case is not made out where there is evidence only that the defendant was under the influence of an intoxicant. To sustain a conviction the evidence must go further: it must be shown that he was under the influence to such an extent as to be incapable of having proper control of his vehicle. Consequently, it may not be enough for a garda to say that the defendant smelled of intoxicating liquor, spoke with a slurred voice and was unsteady on his feet. A court will be more easily persuaded that the defendant was unfit to drive where he is shown to have been unable to perform simple co-ordination tests, such as walking in a straight line. However, before the result of any such test is given in evidence, the prosecution must establish that the defendant voluntarily underwent the test.[13] So long as the defendant is properly cautioned and consents to being medically examined, it is not necessary to inform him of the precise nature of the tests which it is proposed to use.[14]

2.05 The evidence of the doctor and others The question of the evidence permitted to be given by a doctor in the case of a charge under section 49(1) was considered by the High Court in *Director of Public Prosecutions v. Kenny*.[15] Having been arrested for drunken driving, a blood sample was taken from the defendant but no analysis was ever made of it. He was, however, prosecuted for an offence under section 49(1). At the

---

12 *Attorney General (Ruddy) v. Kenny* (1960) 94 ILTR 185. 'Drunkenness, unfortunately, is a condition which is not so exceptional or so much outside the experience of the ordinary individual, that it should require an expert to diagnose it. In my opinion a garda witness, or an ordinary witness, may give evidence of his opinion as to whether a person is drunk or not' — *per* Davitt P in the High Court (at p. 187 of the report) whose judgment was upheld on appeal to the Supreme Court.

13 *Sullivan v. Robinson* [1954] IR 161; (1954) 88 ILTR 169.

14 *Attorney General (Crotty) v. O'Keeffe* [1955] IR 24.

15 [1992] 2 IR 141.

hearing it was submitted that the doctor who had taken the sample could not give evidence either of his observation of the defendant or of his fitness to drive on the grounds (1) that such evidence was obtained in breach of the defendant's constitutional right to privacy and (2) that he should have been cautioned that such evidence might be tendered at the hearing of any charge against him. In his judgment Barron J accepted that the defendant does have a right to privacy while in custody, but held[16] that '(t)his right . . . is not breached by observation of the accused by persons who are lawfully required to deal with him while in custody'. The judge pointed out that the defendant in the case had consented to giving a sample of his blood; therefore he thought it was 'perfectly permissible for the doctor to give evidence of his observation of the accused incidental to the taking of that sample'. The decision in *Kenny* does not, it should be noted, overrule the earlier authorities which require that a test be shown to have been voluntary before its result is given in evidence; *Kenny* merely affirms that persons lawfully dealing with the defendant may give evidence of their observations of him.

2.06 A similar conclusion, but without adverting to the constitutional issue, had been reached over twenty years earlier in *Attorney General (Enright) v. Reilly*.[17] Again the defendant was charged with an offence under section 49(1). He had been brought to a garda station where he was told that he would be examined by a garda doctor, that he was not bound to submit to the examination, but that if he did the findings of the doctor would be given in evidence. The defendant refused to submit to an examination by the garda doctor, who did not carry out an examination, but was called to give evidence for the prosecution. He gave evidence that the defendant's eyes were bloodshot, his speech was slurred, there was a smell of alcohol from his breath, he staggered and was unsteady on his feet. His conclusion was that the defendant was unfit to drive, but he was uncertain as to the cause of that unfitness, other than that the defendant had a smell of alcohol from his breath. On a case stated to the High Court it was asked whether (1) the garda doctor's observation of the defendant amounted to an examination of him and (2) if it did, whether his conclusions based on it were admissible in evidence. Henchy J held that the observation by the doctor did not, in the circumstances, amount to an examination; his evidence 'amounted to no more than that of an observing bystander who happened to be a doctor'. But he also held that, notwithstanding that

---

16 At p. 144 of the report.
17 Unreported judgment of the High Court (Henchy J) delivered 30 January 1967.

the doctor's observation did not amount to a formal medical examination, his account of that observation and his conclusions based on it were admissible in evidence. 'The effect of *Attorney General (Ruddy) v. Kenny*,'[18] said Henchy J,[19] 'is that any witness who has had an opportunity of observing an accused may give evidence of what he observed of the accused's condition, and may give evidence of the opinion he formed from these observations as to the capacity or incapacity of the accused of having proper control of a mechanically propelled vehicle.'

DRIVING WHILE THE CONCENTRATION OF ALCOHOL IN BLOOD OR URINE EXCEEDS THE PERMITTED LEVELS: SECTION 49(2) AND (3) OF THE 1961 ACT

2.07 Most charges of drunken driving are nowadays brought under section 49(2) or (3) for driving when the blood/alcohol or urine/alcohol level exceeds the prescribed limit. In short, the prosecution must prove that the defendant drove a vehicle while the concentration of alcohol in his blood exceeded 80 milligrammes of alcohol per 100 millilitres of blood in the case of a charge under section 49(2), or 107 milligrammes of alcohol per 100 millilitres of urine in the case of a charge under section 49(3). Apart from the different concentrations, the elements of these offences and the procedures to be followed are identical. The elements of the offences may be summarised as follows:

1. There must be evidence that the defendant drove or attempted to drive.[20]

2. There must be evidence that the defendant drove or attempted to drive a mechanically propelled vehicle.[21]

3. There must be evidence that the driving or attempting to drive took place in a public place.[22]

4. There must be evidence that the concentration of alcohol in the defendant's blood or urine exceeded the permitted level within three hours of driving or attempting to drive. The alcohol level may be proved by the production in court of a certificate of analysis from the Medical Bureau of Road Safety.[23]

2.08 The 80 blood alcohol limit This new limit was introduced by the Road Traffic Act 1994, the old limit under its predecessor, the Road

---

18 Supra.
19 At p. 4 of the judgment.
20 See paras. 2.09-2.11 infra.
21 See paras. 2.12-2.14 infra.
22 See paras. 2.15-2.16 infra.
23 See chapter 5.

Traffic (Amendment) Act 1978, having been 100. By reducing the limit to 80 Ireland now has the same limit as that in Belgium, Denmark, Luxembourg, France, Germany, Italy, Spain and the United Kingdom. A lower limit of 50 applies in the other European Union states, Greece, the Netherlands and Portugal. Apart from keeping in line with the law in other European states, the reduction in the permitted limit was justified by the Minister for the Environment by reference to evidence showing that alcohol is a factor in a significant number of road accidents. He cited[24] international studies showing that between 25 and 50 per cent of all road accidents can be attributed to alcohol, though he suggested that the figure for Ireland was 33 per cent. Excessive alcohol in the blood results, he said, in impairment of peripheral vision and the eye's reaction to light and dark; judgment of distance and speed and ability to react are adversely affected and excessive consumption gives rise to a tendency to take risks. The Minister referred[25] to American studies which show that at 100 milligrammes of alcohol per 100 millilitres of blood one is twice as likely to have an accident as with zero alcohol, and at 200 milligrammes one is 25 times as likely.

DRIVING OR ATTEMPTING TO DRIVE

2.09 A defendant may be charged that he did on the occasion in question 'drive or attempt to drive'; however, a simple conviction on such a charge would be bad for uncertainty, the proper course being to convict of one or other of the offences charged.[26] The fact of driving may be proved by the testimony of a witness or witnesses or other admissible evidence. In many cases it is proved by the admission of the defendant to a member of the Garda Síochána.[27] An admission of driving must, of course, have been made voluntarily before it is admissible in evidence.[28] Where a garda has made up his mind to charge a defendant with drunken driving, then he should under the Judges' Rules administer a caution before asking him any questions.[29] The absence of a caution in such circumstances does not of itself render an admission of driving inadmissible: it gives rise to a

---

24 139 Seanad Debates 871-872.
25 139 Seanad Debates 872.
26 *State (Taylor) v. The Circuit Court Judge for the County of Wicklow* [1951] IR 311.
27 See section 107 of the 1961 Act which empowers a garda to demand the name and address of the user of a mechanically propelled vehicle.
28 *McCarrick v. Leavy* [1964] IR 225; (1965) 99 ILTR 163.
29 See 'Admissibility of a Statement Without a Caution in a Drunk Driving Case', (1985) 3 ILT (NS) 126.

discretion in the trial judge to refuse to admit the evidence.[30] But the absence of a caution does require an explanation, and the explanation offered is to be taken into consideration by the trial judge before exercising his discretion.[31]

2.10 There is little in the way of Irish authority as to what actually constitutes 'driving'. The 1961 Act, section 3(1), merely provides that '"driving" includes managing and controlling'. In Britain there have been many cases on the point.[32] The Court of Appeal in *R. v. McDonagh*[33] has held that:

> The essence of driving is the use of the driver's controls in order to direct the movement, however that movement is produced. We would draw attention to . . . two factors . . .: first, that the alleged driver must be in the driving seat, or in control of the steering wheel; and, secondly, that his activities are nevertheless not to be held to amount to driving unless they come within the ordinary meaning of that word.

In *Edkins v. Knowles*[34] a divisional court of the High Court considered the authorities and summarised their effect as follows:

1. The vehicle does not have to be in motion; there will always be a brief interval of time after the vehicle has been brought to rest and before the motorist has completed those operations necessarily connected with driving, such as applying the handbrake, switching off the ignition and securing the vehicle, during which he must still be considered to be driving.

2. When a motorist stops before he has completed his journey he may still be driving; an obvious example is when he is halted at traffic lights. Each case will depend upon its own facts, but generally the following questions will be relevant: (a) What was the purpose of the stop? If it is connected with the driving, and not for some purpose unconnected with the driving, the facts may justify a finding that the driving is continuing although the vehicle is stationary. (b) How long was he stopped? The longer he is stopped the more difficult it becomes to regard him as still driving. (c) Did he get out of the vehicle? If he remains in the vehicle it is some though not a conclusive indication that he is still driving.

---

30 *McCarrick v. Leavy*, supra.
31 *People (DPP) v. Farrell* [1978] IR 13.
32 See *Wilkinson's Road Traffic Offences*, 16th edition, (London, 1993), paras. 1.129-1.136.
33 [1974] RTR 372, 374-375 per Lord Widgery CJ.
34 [1973] RTR 257, 262-263.

3. If a motorist is stopped by a constable in uniform who immediately forms the suspicion that the motorist has alcohol in his body, the motorist should be regarded as still driving at the moment when the suspicion is formed: but if an appreciable time elapses before the constable's suspicion is aroused it will be a question of fact and degree whether the motorist is still to be considered as driving at that time.

4. When a motorist has arrived at the end of his journey then subject to the brief interval referred to in 1 above he can no longer be regarded as driving.

5. When a motorist has been effectively prevented or persuaded from driving he can no longer be considered to be driving.

2.11 The question whether there had been an attempt to drive was considered by the High Court in *State (Prendergast) v. Porter*.[35] The defendant was charged with attempting to drive a mechanically propelled vehicle while drunk. The evidence disclosed that the defendant had gone to the front of the vehicle and commenced to turn what appeared to be the starting handle. He then went to the right-hand side of the vehicle and, having opened the door, leaned into the cabin and seemed to touch the dashboard instruments. The defendant returned to the front of the vehicle and again turned the starting handle. He then sat on the driving seat and the engine turned over but did not start. The District Justice found that the defendant had the immediate intention of driving the vehicle. On a case stated it was held that the defendant's actions amounted to an attempt to drive and that the District Justice was wrong in dismissing the charge.

A MECHANICALLY PROPELLED VEHICLE

2.12 A 'mechanically propelled vehicle' is defined in section 3(1) of the 1961 Act as 'a vehicle intended or adapted for propulsion by mechanical means, including—(a) a bicycle or tricycle with an attachment for propelling it by mechanical power, whether or not the attachment is being used, (b) a vehicle the means of propulsion of which is electrical or partly electrical and partly mechanical, but not including a tramcar or other vehicle running on permanent rails'. The term 'vehicle' is not itself defined in the legislation. In *Boxer v. Snelling*[36] it was held that, in determining in

---

35 [1961] Ir Jur Rep 14.   36 [1972] RTR 472.

a borderline case whether a contrivance is a vehicle, a court may have regard not only to its construction, nature and function, but also to the circumstances in which it is used.

2.13 Ordinarily proof that the defendant was driving a mechanically propelled vehicle poses no great difficulty. The investigating garda will give evidence that the defendant admitted driving a motor car bearing a particular registration number or a witness can describe the vehicle driven on the occasion. However, there may be difficulty where, for example, a garda on arrival at the scene of an accident finds the defendant in charge of a badly damaged car. Here the question may arise whether the car is still a mechanically propelled vehicle. Section 3(2) of the 1961 Act provides that: 'Where a vehicle, which, apart from this subsection, would be a mechanically propelled vehicle, stands so substantially disabled (either through accident, breakdown or the removal of the engine or other such vital part) as to be no longer capable of being propelled mechanically, it shall be regarded for the purposes of this Act as not being a mechanically propelled vehicle.'

2.14 The question whether a damaged car was a mechanically propelled vehicle was considered in *Director of Public Prosecutions v. Breheny*.[37] Here the defendant's car had struck another car and the defendant then tried to drive away. However, the evidence was that only the starting motor came on and, on each attempt to start the car, it jumped but would not drive. It was held in the District Court that in these circumstances the car was not a mechanically propelled vehicle and in the Supreme Court Egan J expressed the view that this was correct. In Northern Ireland it has been held that a car with a flat battery is still a motor vehicle.[38] And in England it has been held that a moped does not cease to be a motor vehicle merely because it suffers a temporary loss of engine power.[39] But where the cylinder and piston had been removed from an auto-cycle it was held to be a pedal cycle rather than a motor vehicle.[40]

A PUBLIC PLACE

2.15 The term 'public place' is now defined[41] as '(a) any public road, and

---

37 Unreported decision of the Supreme Court, judgment delivered 2 March 1993.
38 *R. v. Paul* [1952] NI 61.
39 *R. v. Tashin* [1970] RTR 88.
40 *Lawrence v. Howlett* [1952] 2 All ER 74.
41 In section 3(1) of the Road Traffic Act

(b) any street, road or other place to which the public have access with vehicles whether as of right or by permission and whether subject to or free of charge'. The old definition of public place in the 1961 Act contained only the words after (b), 'any street, road, etc.'; the 1994 Act amended the definition by the addition of '(a) any public road'. The necessity for this amendment arose from the decision of the High Court in *Director of Public Prosecutions v Molloy*[42] where the issue was whether Grafton Street in Dublin, at a time when it was pedestrianised and so closed to motor vehicles, was a public place for the purpose of offences under the Road Traffic Acts. Murphy J held that since vehicular access to the street was prohibited under the Dublin Traffic and Parking Temporary Rules, 1982 (SI No. 109 of 1982), Grafton Street did not at the time of the alleged offences come within the statutory definition in the 1961 Act.[43] The 1961 Act definition was also considered by the High Court in *Attorney General (McLoughlin) v. Rhatigan*[44] where it was held that the onus lay on the prosecution to prove that the offence was committed in a public place, and that to prove that a place is a public place within the meaning of the Act the prosecution must establish the fact that the public has a right of access to it. In that case the evidence was that the place was a 'private' car park and that there were two other vehicles in the place as well as the defendant's. It was held that this evidence was insufficient to show that the public had access to the place, and so the prosecution had failed to show that the place was a public one.

2.16 In the course of his judgment in *Director of Public Prosecutions v. Molloy*[45] Murphy J approved the following dictum of Lord MacDermott LCJ in *Montgomery v. Loney*:[46] 'There can be little doubt that the main object which Parliament had in mind in enacting these provisions was the protection of members of the community from the dangers of road traffic and, in particular, from those caused by motor vehicles. That has to be borne in mind in construing "public" and "access", for these words have no fixed and inflexible meaning and their true signification must depend on their context and the purpose for which they are used.' The issue in *Montgomery v. Loney* was whether the forecourt of a filling station was a

1961 as substituted by section 49(1)(a)(iv) of the Road Traffic Act 1994.
42 [1994] 1 IR 583; [1993] ILRM 573.
43 This paradoxical conclusion is under appeal to the Supreme Court.
44 (1966) 100 ILTR 37. See also *Attorney General (Doyle) v. Farrell* (1954) 88 ILTR 174.
45 Supra.
46 [1959] NI 171, 176.

'road or other public place' for the purposes of the Road Traffic Act (Northern Ireland), 1955. Lord MacDermott LCJ[47] in his judgment reached the following conclusions with regard to the definition of a 'road' in the 1955 Act. It is submitted that they would apply with equal force to the definition of a 'public place' in the 1961 Act.

> In so far as relevant to this appeal I would now restate my conclusions on the definition of 'road' in section 75 of that Act as follows:
>
> 1. As respects private property, 'access' means access by permission, either express or to be implied from acquiescence or other conduct on the part of the owner or occupier. It does not mean access in fact and irrespective of the will of the owner or occupier.
> 2. 'The public' means the public at large or a substantial section thereof. What constitutes a substantial section for this purpose must be determined with regard to the relevant circumstances and the dominant object of the statute, namely, the protection of the public. Generally, the decision will be a matter of fact and degree, but whether the material for consideration suffices to support one view or the other is a matter of law.
> 3. But those who are allowed to enter private property, not as members of the public, but for reasons in some way personal to the individuals admitted, will not be regarded as the general public or a substantial section thereof, and their admission will not constitute the giving of access to the public for the purposes of the definition. Pass holders entering a dock area, or employees going to work along a factory road, for example, do not bring the definition into play because they obtain access, not as members of the public, but on the strength of a relationship between the individual and the owner or occupier concerned.

DRUNK IN CHARGE: SECTION 50 OF THE 1961 ACT

2.17 The offence of being drunk in charge of a mechanically propelled vehicle is dealt with in section 50 of the 1961 Act as substituted by section 11 of the 1994 Act. The offences created by section 50 correspond to the offences under section 49 save that they apply to a person 'in charge of a mechanically propelled vehicle in a public place with intent to drive or

---

47 At pp. 186-187 of the report.

attempt to drive the vehicle (but not driving or attempting to drive it)'.[48] Thus section 50(1)(a) makes it an offence to be in charge of a mechanically propelled vehicle in a public place with the requisite intent while under the influence of an intoxicant to such an extent as to be incapable of having proper control of the vehicle. Section 50(2) makes it an offence to be in charge while there is present in the person's body a quantity of alcohol such that, within three hours after having been in charge, the concentration of alcohol in the blood exceeds a concentration of 80 milligrammes of alcohol per 100 millilitres of blood. Section 50(3) makes it an offence to be in charge while there is present in the person's body a quantity of alcohol such that, within three hours after having been in charge, the concentration of alcohol in the urine exceeds a concentration of 107 milligrammes of alcohol per 100 millilitres of urine. And section 50(4) makes it an offence to be in charge while there is present in the person's body a quantity of alcohol such that, within three hours after having been in charge, the concentration alcohol in the breath exceeds a concentration of 35 microgrammes of alcohol per 100 millilitres of breath.

2.18   In a prosecution for an offence under section 50 it is presumed that the defendant intended to drive or attempt to drive until he shows the contrary.[49] And in a prosecution for an offence under section 50(1) it is not a good defence for the defendant to show that an analysis has not been carried out or that he was not requested to provide a breath specimen.[50] A person charged with an offence under section 50 may, in lieu of being found guilty of that offence, be found guilty of an offence under section 49.[51]

2.19   The term 'in charge' is not defined in the legislation. Whether a person is 'in charge' is a question of fact to be determined from the circumstances of each individual case. In Northern Ireland it has been held that a defendant who did not have his ignition key and was found lying on the footpath with his head and shoulders on the front passenger seat of his car was in charge.[52] So too was a person who had his key and was approaching his vehicle but was arrested before he could get into it.[53]

---

48   See paras. 2.12-2.14 supra with regard to the meaning of a 'mechanically propelled vehicle' and paras. 2.15-2.16 supra with regard to the meaning of a 'public place'.
49   Section 50(8) of the 1961 Act as inserted by section 11 of the 1994 Act.
50   Section 24 of the 1994 Act.
51   Section 50(6)(b) of the 1961 Act as inserted by section 11 of the 1994 Act.
52   *Walker v. Rountree* [1963] NI 23.
53   *Leach v. Evans* [1952] 2 All ER 264.

However, in at least one English case a person found in a car sleeping off the effects of drink has escaped conviction.[54] In *Director of Public Prosecutions v Watkins*[55] a divisional court of the High Court laid down the following principles for the purpose of determining whether the defendant is 'in charge':

> (1) If the defendant is the owner or lawful possessor of the vehicle or has recently driven it, he will have been in charge of it, and the question for the court will be whether he is still in charge or whether he has relinquished his charge. . . . Usually such a defendant will be prima facie in charge unless he has put the vehicle in someone else's charge. However he would not be so if in all the circumstances he has ceased to be in actual control and there is no realistic possibility of his resuming actual control while unfit, eg, if he is at home in bed for the night, or if he is a great distance from the car or if it is taken by another.
>
> (2) If the defendant is not the owner, the lawful possessor or recent driver but is sitting in the vehicle or is otherwise involved with it, the question for the court is . . . whether he has assumed being in charge of it. In this class of case the defendant will be in charge if, whilst unfit, he is voluntarily in de facto control of the vehicle or if, in the circumstances, including his position, his intentions and his actions, he may be expected imminently to assume control. Usually this will involve his having gained entry to the car and evinced an intention to take control of it. But gaining entry may not be necessary if he has manifested that intention some other way, eg, by stealing the keys of a car in circumstances which show he means presently to drive it. The circumstances to be taken into account will vary infinitely but the following will usually be relevant: (i) whether and where he is in the vehicle or how far he is from it; (ii) what he is doing at the relevant time; (iii) whether he is in possession of a key that fits the ignition; (iv) whether there is evidence of an intention to take or assert control of the car by driving or otherwise; (v) whether any other person is in, at or near the vehicle and if so, the like particulars in respect of that person.

---

54 *Williams v. Osborne* [1975] RTR 181.   55 [1989] RTR 324, 331.

FRUSTRATING A PROSECUTION AND THE 'HIP FLASK' DEFENCE: SECTION 20 OF THE 1994 ACT

2.20 On the hearing of a charge under sections 49 or 50 it is not necessary to show that the defendant had not consumed intoxicating liquor after the time when the offence is alleged to have been committed but before the taking or provision of the specimen.[56] But where, in such a case, evidence is given by or on behalf of the defendant that, after the time when the offence is alleged to have been committed but before the taking or provision of the specimen, he had consumed intoxicating liquor, the court must disregard the evidence unless satisfied that, but for that consumption, the concentration of alcohol in the defendant's blood, urine or breath would not have exceeded the appropriate prescribed limit.[57] A person who takes or attempts to take any action (including consumption of alcohol, but excluding a refusal or failure to provide a specimen of his breath, urine or blood) with the intention of frustrating a prosecution under sections 49 or 50 is guilty of an offence.[58] And where, on the hearing of a charge for an offence under sections 49 or 50, the court is satisfied that such action taken by the defendant was taken with the intention of frustrating a prosecution under those sections, the court may find him guilty of the offence.[59] The purpose of section 20 is to deprive a defendant of the so-called 'hip flask' defence. It does so by casting the onus on him of showing that the intoxicating liquor consumed by him after he was stopped put him over the prescribed limit; it would appear that, if he fails to adduce any evidence as to the effect of the alcohol consumed after he was stopped on the result of the analysis, then he must be convicted assuming the analysis shows that the concentration exceeded the prescribed limit and the other statutory requirements are complied with. Section 20 is, however, of less assistance to the prosecution in a case brought under section 49(1) or section 50(1): it only requires the court to disregard the drink taken from the hip flask 'before the taking or provision of a the specimen'. So in a case where no specimen is taken, the issue of the accused's fitness to drive may be confused by evidence of his consumption of alcohol after being apprehended.

---

56 Section 20(1) of the 1994 Act.
57 Section 20(2) of the 1994 Act.
58 Section 20(3) of the 1994 Act.
59 Section 20(4) of the 1994 Act.

PERSONS UNDER THE INFLUENCE OF DRUGS AND THE OBLIGATION TO PROVIDE A SPECIMEN: SECTION 14 OF THE 1994 ACT

2.21 Section 14 of the 1994 deals with a garda's powers in the case of a person under the influence of drugs. Apart from his powers to arrest any person who has driven or is in charge of a mechanically propelled vehicle while under the influence of an intoxicant[60] (a term defined so as to include 'drugs and any combination of drugs or of drugs and alcohol'), a member of the Garda Síochána, if of the opinion that a person in charge of a mechanically propelled vehicle in a public place is under the influence of a drug or drugs to the extent as to be incapable of having proper control of the vehicle, may require the person to accompany him to a garda station.[61] Refusal or failure to comply with this requirement is an offence.[62] A garda may arrest without warrant a person who in his opinion is committing or has committed this offence.[63] It is noteworthy that section 14 does not contemplate an arrest where a garda is of the opinion that the person is under the influence of drugs: instead the person is obliged to accompany the garda to a garda station: the power of arrest only arises where there has been a refusal or failure to fulfil this obligation.

2.22 Once in the garda station a member of the Garda Síochána may require the person to permit a designated doctor to take from him a specimen of his blood or, at the option of the person, provide for the designated doctor a specimen of his urine.[64] If the doctor states in writing that he is unwilling, on medical grounds, to take from the person or be provided by him with the specimen to which the requirement related, the garda may require the person to furnish a specimen other than to which the first requirement related.[65] Refusal or failure to comply with the requirement of the garda, or to comply with a requirement of a designated doctor in relation to the taking or provision of a specimen, is an offence.[66]

60 Under sections 49(8) and 50(10) of the 1961 Act as inserted by sections 10 and 11 of the 1994 Act respectively.
61 Section 14(1) of the 1994 Act.
62 Section 14(2) of the 1994 Act.
63 Section 14(3) of the 1994 Act.
64 Section 14(4) of the 1994 Act.
65 Ibid.
66 Section 14(5) of the 1994 Act; although in a prosecution for refusing or failing to comply with a requirement to permit a designated doctor to take a specimen of blood or for refusing or failing to comply with his requirement in relation to the taking of a specimen of blood, it is a defence for the defendant to show that there was a special and substantial reason for the refusal or failure and that he complied (or offered, but was not called upon, to comply) with a requirement in relation to the provision of a specimen of urine: see para. 4.07 post.

The procedure to be followed after the specimen has been furnished is essentially the same as in the case of a specimen taken from of a driver under the influence of alcohol, save of course that the bureau will analyse for drugs.[67]

---

67 See sections 18 and 19 of the 1994 Act and chapter 4.

3

The Statutory Procedure in Drunken Driving Cases: Part 1

THE STATUTORY FORMAT

3.01 The road traffic legislation lays down a statutory format for prosecutions for drunken driving and being drunk in charge. It is as follows:

1. A garda may breathalyse a person in charge of a mechanically propelled vehicle in a public place if of the opinion that the person has consumed intoxicating liquor: section 12(1) of the 1994 Act.

2. A person who refuses or fails to comply with this requirement is guilty of an offence and may be arrested: section 12(2) and (3) of the 1994 Act.

3. Where the garda forms the opinion that the person has committed an offence under sections 49 or 50, he may arrest him: section 49(8) of the 1961 Act as inserted by section 10 of the 1994 Act and section 50(10) of the 1961 Act as inserted by section 11 of the 1994 Act.

4. After the arrested person has been brought to a garda station, a garda may, at his discretion, require him to do either or both of the following: (a) provide two specimens of his breath by exhaling into an apparatus for determining the concentration of alcohol in the breath or (b) permit a designated doctor to take a specimen of his blood or, at the option of the person, provide for the designated doctor a specimen of his urine: section 13(1) of the 1994 Act.

5. Refusal or failure to comply with the garda's requirement, or to comply with a requirement of the designated doctor in relation to the taking or provision of the blood or urine specimen, is an offence: sections 13(2) and (3) of the 1994 Act.

6. After a blood or urine specimen[1] has been provided the designated doctor

---

[1] The apparatus for the provision of breath specimens in the garda station (as distinct from the preliminary breath test or 'breathalyser' used at the roadside) has not yet been

must divide it into two parts, place each in a container which he must seal forthwith, and complete the prescribed form: section 18(1) of the 1994 Act.

7. After the specimen has been divided into two parts a garda must offer one of the sealed containers to the person together with a statement in writing indicating that he may retain either of them: section 18(2) of the 1994 Act.

8. A garda must then, as soon as practicable, cause the completed doctor's form together with one of the sealed containers, or both of them, where the person has declined to retain one, to be forwarded to the Medical Bureau of Road Safety: section 18(3) of the 1994 Act.

9. The bureau must analyse the specimen and determine the concentration of alcohol as soon as practicable after it has received it: section 19(1) of the 1994 Act.

10. The bureau must then, as soon as practicable, forward a completed certificate in the prescribed form to the garda station from which the specimen was forwarded and a copy of the completed certificate to the person named on the doctor's form as the person from whom the specimen was taken: section 19(3) of the 1994 Act.

11. The duly completed doctor's form and the bureau's certificate are sufficient evidence of the facts stated in them until the contrary is shown: section 21(2) and (3) of the 1994 Act.

3.02 Generally all of the elements in the format are essential in order to sustain a conviction. In the words of O'Higgins CJ:[2]

> Where a statute provides for a particular form of proof or evidence in compliance with certain statutory provisions, in my view it is essential that the precise statutory provisions be complied with. The Courts cannot accept something other than that which is laid down by the statute, or overlook the absence of what the statute requires.

---

introduced: the steps to be followed when the apparatus is utilised are outlined in paras. 4.22-4.23 post.

2   Albeit in a dissenting judgment: *Director of Public Prosecutions v. Kemmy* [1980] IR 160, 164. See also the judgment of Denham J in *Director of Public Prosecutions v. Fanagan*, unreported judgment of the High Court delivered 18 December 1991: 'The statute (referring to the 1978 Act) should be interpreted reasonably but strictly, as it is a penal statute and as it affects the fundamental rights of the person.'

To do so would be to trespass into the legislative field. This applies to all statutory requirements; but it applies with greater general understanding to penal statutes which create particular offences and then provide a particular method for their proof. The Act of 1978 (now 1994) is a penal statute.

One element in the statutory format is not essential: there is no obligation on an investigating garda to breathalyse a suspect before he effects an arrest for drunken driving or being drunk in charge;[3] although, of course, if he does do so, there is less likelihood that the validity of the arrest can be challenged. Proof of other elements in the statutory format is dispensed with by a number of presumptions laid down in the 1994 Act. Thus section 18(4) provides that it is presumed that subsections (1) to (3) in that section (elements 6-8 above) have been complied with. Section 21(3) provides that the bureau's certificate is 'sufficient evidence of compliance by the Bureau with the requirements imposed on it by or under this Part or Part V of the Act of 1968' (elements 9 and 10 above). And section 21(4) provides that a person who, by virtue of a power conferred on him by Part III of the Act, took from another a specimen of his blood or was provided by another with a specimen of his urine is presumed to be a designated doctor. All of these presumptions are rebuttable. If the prosecution fails to prove an element in the statutory format which it is required to prove, the court may reject its case for that reason alone, or because the defect in its case affects the validity and admissibility of some essential proof,[4] or because the prosecution case has become tainted with illegality.[5]

THE DETECTION OF OFFENCES

3.03 A prosecution for drunken driving may result from a traffic accident when a garda, having interviewed a driver involved, forms an opinion as to his condition, perhaps breathalyses him and then effects an arrest. Likewise a prosecution may stem from a garda's observations of a driver asked to stop at a checkpoint. Until the decision in *Director of Public Prosecutions (Stratford) v. Fagan*[6] it was questionable whether a garda was

---

3   *Director of Public Prosecutions v. Donoghue* [1986] IR 188; [1987] ILRM 129.
4   As in *People (DPP) v. Greeley* [1985] ILRM 320; see para. 3.10 infra.
5   As in *Director of Public Prosecutions v. Joyce* [1985] ILRM 206; see para. 3.06 infra.
6   [1994] 2 ILRM 349. See also *Director of Public Prosecutions v. Cowman* [1993] 1 IR 335, 337 where O'Hanlon J rejected the view that there is a 're-

empowered to conduct checks by stopping drivers at random. The Road Traffic Acts did not explicitly confer such a power on him; section 109(1) of the 1961 Act, as amended by the schedule to the 1968 Act, provided only that 'A person driving a vehicle in a public place shall stop the vehicle on being so required by a member of the Garda Síochána and shall keep it stationary for such period as is reasonably necessary in order to enable such member to discharge his duties.'

3.04 In *Fagan* the defendant was stopped when driving along Cathal Brugha Street in Dublin by a garda on checkpoint duty. On speaking to the defendant the garda got a smell of intoxicating liquor from his breath and his speech was slurred, and when the defendant got out of his car he was unsteady. Having formed the opinion that the defendant was under the influence of intoxicating liquor to such an extent as to render him incapable of having proper control of a mechanically propelled vehicle in a public place, the garda arrested him for drunken driving. In the District Court the question arose whether a garda, who does not suspect an offence, is entitled to stop a driver. On a case stated to the High Court it was decided that he did, a decision upheld on appeal to the Supreme Court. The gardaí, it was held, are empowered to check motor vehicles in the performance of their duty to detect or prevent crime, subject to the caveat that the 'power to stop must be exercised (like all powers) not in a capricious manner but in a constant fashion and with due civility and courtesy'.[7]

---

striction . . . imposed by the law on the right of a member of the Garda Síochána to approach members of the public from time to time as he thinks fit for the purpose of speaking to them and having communication with them on an informal basis.'

7 P. 355 of the report *per* O'Flaherty J. In an interesting and strong dissenting judgment Denham J expressed the view (at p. 368 of the report) that 'It would be contrary to the fundamental principles of personal rights under the Constitution, the rule of law, and the initiation of a concept with far reaching consequences, to justify the action of the garda on the basis that he was "on duty". The logical sequel would be that all actions performed "on duty" would be legal and permitted. It would establish an authority, based on a broad concept of duty, which is unclear and uncertain. Ultimately this is of benefit neither to the gardaí nor citizens.' Certainly Denham J would appear to be right that the decision of the majority of the Supreme Court marks a new departure in the attitude of the courts to the powers of the police.

THE BREATHALYSER

3.05 Under section 12(1)(a) of the 1994 Act a member of the Garda Síochána may, whenever he is of the opinion that a person in charge of a mechanically propelled vehicle in a public place has consumed intoxicating liquor, require the person to provide a specimen of his breath by exhaling into an apparatus for indicating the presence of alcohol in the breath.[8] The garda may indicate the manner in which the person is to comply with the requirement.[9] He may also require the person to accompany him to a place (including a vehicle) at or in the vicinity of the public place and require him to provide a breath specimen there.[10] If the garda does not have an apparatus with him, he may require the person to remain at the place in his presence or in the presence of another garda until such time (but for no longer than one hour) until an apparatus becomes available whereupon he may then require the provision of the specimen.[11] Refusal or failure to comply forthwith with the requirement of a garda made under section 12, or to comply forthwith in the manner indicated by him, is an offence.[12] A garda may arrest without warrant a person who in his opinion is committing or has committed an offence under the section.[13] It has been held that a garda making a requirement under section 12 is not obliged to inform the person of the particular section under which the requirement is made nor is he obliged to inform him of the consequences of a refusal or failure to comply.[14]

3.06 The circumstances in which a breathalyser may be administered The power to administer a breathalyser is subject to the limitations imposed by the terms of section 12. 'The power may only be exercised,' as O'Hanlon J pointed out in *Director of Public Prosecutions v. Brady*,[15] 'in accordance with the requirements of the section when the garda exercising

---

8 In a prosecution for an offence under part III of the 1994 Act or under section 49 or 50 of the 1961 Act it is presumed, until the contrary is shown, that an apparatus provided by a member of the Garda Síochána for the purpose of enabling a person to provide a specimen of breath pursuant to section 12 is an apparatus for indicating the presence of alcohol in the breath: section 12(4) of the 1994 Act.
9 Section 12(1)(a) of the 1994 Act.
10 Section 12(1)(b) of the 1994 Act.
11 Section 12(1)(c) of the 1994 Act.
12 Section 12(2) of the 1994 Act.
13 Section 12(3) of the 1994 Act.
14 *Director of Public Prosecutions v. Gaughran* [1993] 3 IR 598. This decision arose out of a prosecution for an offence under section 49(2), and it was acknowledged that in a prosecution for refusal or failure under section 12 different considerations might apply.
15 [1991] 1 IR 337, 339 and see para. 3.07 infra.

it has first formed the opinion that the person concerned has consumed intoxicating liquor. I agree with the view taken by the learned District Justice that this does not arise as a necessary inference from the fact that he has stopped a driver and required him to undergo the test.' Before a breath test is administered the defendant must, under section 12, be 'a person in charge of a mechanically propelled vehicle in a public place'. In *Director of Public Prosecutions v. Joyce*[16] it was held that a breath test administered in a private yard owned by the defendant, which proved positive and which the garda relied on to arrest the defendant, was improper and tainted with illegality everything done thereafter.

3.07 Whether the garda must give evidence of his opinion
Although a garda must have the opinion required by section 12 before administering a breathalyser, it was decided in *Director of Public Prosecutions v. Brady*[17] that in a prosecution under section 49(2) as inserted by the 1978 Act it was not necessary for him to give formal proof of that opinion. So long as the evidence shows that there is a basis in fact justifying the opinion, it is not an essential proof in a prosecution under section 49 for the garda to say explicitly in evidence that he formed the opinion that the defendant had consumed intoxicating liquor.

3.08 The significance of a positive breath test A positive breath test, it has been held,[18] is sufficient to justify an opinion on the part of a garda who carries out the test that an offence under section 49(2) or 49(3) has been committed. It does not, of itself, justify an opinion that there has been an offence under section 49(1).[19] But if a garda says that, as a result of the positive breathalyser, he formed the opinion that the defendant had consumed an intoxicant to such an extent as to be incapable of having proper control of his vehicle, a court will infer that he had the appropriate opinion, that is to say, that the concentration of alcohol in the defendant's blood or urine exceeded the prescribed limit.[20]

3.09 The apparatus and whether it must be produced in court By virtue of section 12(4) of the 1994 Act there is a presumption that 'an apparatus provided by a member of the Garda Síochána for the purpose

16 [1985] ILRM 206.
17 Supra.
18 *Director of Public Prosecutions v. Gilmore* [1981] ILRM 102.
19 *Director of Public Prosecutions v. Donoghue* [1986] IR 188; [1987] ILRM 129.
20 *Director of Public Prosecutions v. Gilmore*, supra.

of enabling a person to provide a specimen of breath pursuant to this section is an apparatus for indicating the the presence of alcohol in the breath'. In *State (Murray) v. Clifford*[21] it was held that generally there is no requirement that the prosecution produce in court the apparatus by which the breath test was administered. However, it was pointed by Finlay P (as he then was) that:

> If a person were stopped by a member of the Garda Síochána and had a request made to him under section 12 ... and were then offered something which on its appearance or by reason of a patent defect in it could not properly be described as an apparatus for breath testing for alcohol he would have a lawful reason to refuse to submit himself to a test by that apparatus. In that situation it seems to me that he would be in a position to give evidence of the patent defect of the apparatus or of the appearance, construction or design of the apparatus upon which he formed the opinion that it was not an apparatus for breath testing for alcohol which was the foundation of his lawful refusal to submit himself to the test. With such evidence being given it might well be that the failure of the Prosecution witness to produce the actual apparatus which he in fact tendered to the person concerned would so take away from the weight of his evidence that an acquittal would be the result.

THE ARREST

3.10 A garda has a statutory power to arrest without a warrant a person who, in his opinion, is committing or has committed an offence under section 49 of the 1961 Act,[22] section 50 of the 1961 Act,[23] or section 12 of the 1994 Act.[24] It is clear that an arrest is an essential element in a prosecution under section 49(2), (3) or (4). In *People (DPP) v. Greeley*[25] it was accepted by the High Court that where the defendant was not arrested at the place where he had driven, but voluntarily went to the garda station and was subsequently arrested there, there was no power to require him to furnish a specimen under section 13 of the 1978 Act (which

---

21 Unreported judgment of the High Court (Finlay P, as he then was) delivered 4 February 1980.
22 Section 49(8) of the 1961 Act as inserted by section 10 of the 1994 Act.
23 Section 50(10) of the 1961 Act as inserted by section 11 of the 1994 Act.
24 Section 12(3) of the 1994 Act.
25 [1985] ILRM 320.

corresponds but is not identical to section 13 of the 1994 Act). A certificate issued by the bureau in such a case would not, it was held, be admissible in evidence.

3.11 The garda's opinion justifying the arrest To justify an arrest for drunken driving a garda must have the opinion that the defendant is committing or has committed an offence under section 49. But he is not required to have in mind any one of the specific offences created by the section. As Costello J (as he then was) pointed out in the course of his judgment in *Hobbs v. Hurley*:[26]

> There are three distinct offences created by section 49 and it is quite clear that at the time of arrest it would not be possible for the garda then to know under which sub-section a suspect would subsequently be charged. The Oireachtas has therefore permitted an arrest to be made when an opinion is arrived at that an offence under the section has been committed — an opinion which does not depend on a conscious determination based on scientific evidence that the statutory limit of alcohol in the blood or urine of the arrested person has been exceeded.

However, the garda's opinion must be reasonable and must be genuinely held by him. In the words of Costello J:[27]

> The opinion arrived at must, of course, be a reasonable one and must be one which results from an honest belief come to after facts have been ascertained and considered. In the present case Garda Hobbs (the arresting garda) smelled alcohol in the defendant's breath and he noticed that the defendant's eyes were bloodshot. The alkalyser test confirmed the existence of alcohol in the defendant's breath. In reaching a conclusion that an offence under the section had been committed Garda Hobbs was entitled to rely on his own observations alone, or on his own observations aided by the positive finding on the alkalyser test. The fact that he had no positive scientific knowledge as to the extent of the concentration of alcohol in the suspect's urine does not in any way vitiate the opinion which otherwise he had reached.

---

26 Unreported judgment of the High Court (Costello J, as he then was) delivered 10 June 1980 at pp. 4-5 of the judgment.

27 At pp. 5-6 of the judgment; see also *Director of Public Prosecutions v. Donoghue* [1986] IR 188; [1987] ILRM 129.

Innocent explanations for a defendant's appearance and conduct will not deprive an arrest of its validity so long as it is objectively reasonable for a garda to conclude that an offence has been committed. In *Director of Public Prosecutions v. Gray*[28] O'Hanlon J observed that:

> The learned District Justice appears ... to have rejected the evidence of the Garda as unreasonable because it appeared to him (the District Justice) that there were other possible explanations for all the features of the defendant's conduct which were described by the garda in evidence, not necessarily involving over-consumption of alcohol. This, however, could be put forward in every case, no matter what factual evidence led up to an arrest. A person charged may have bloodshot eyes because he has been deprived of sleep for days on end. His speech may be slurred because he has recently undergone complicated dental treatment. He may fall down on the road because of a latent neurological condition having nothing to do with the consumption of alcohol. The list is endless. The fact that a defendant may have a completely convincing explanation for all the matters observed by an arresting garda does not, in my opinion, deprive the arrest of its validity if it was objectively reasonable for the garda to form the opinion that the person concerned is committing or has committed an offence under the section.

As we have seen, failure to pass a breathalyser test is sufficient to justify an arrest.[29]

3.12 Express evidence of the opinion As a general rule there should be express evidence from the arresting garda that he had the requisite opinion. In *Director of Public Prosecutions v. Lynch*[30] a garda on duty at a checkpoint signalled a car to stop. The car braked a good distance from the checkpoint, then drove up to where the garda was standing. The garda observed that the driver 'had a drowsy appearance, his speech was slurred, and that he was unsteady on his feet'. In evidence he said that he formed the opinion that the defendant was incapable of driving a mechanically propelled vehicle in a public place whereupon he arrested him under section 49. The charge was dismissed in the District Court because the garda had

---

28 Unreported judgment of the High Court (O'Hanlon J) delivered 8 May 1987 at pp. 3-4 of the judgment.
29 See para. 3.08 supra and *Director of Public Prosecutions v. Gilmore* [1981] ILRM 102.
30 [1991] 1 IR 43.

failed to give evidence of an adequate opinion validating the arrest. On appeal by case stated to the High Court O'Hanlon J held[31] that in the circumstances of the case 'it was necessary that evidence should have been given of a positive nature that the arresting garda had in fact formed the necessary opinion to validate an arrest under section 49 of the Act.'

3.13   But there are cases where the existence of the requisite opinion on the part of the garda can be inferred from the circumstances. This was established by the Supreme Court in *Director of Public Prosecutions v. O'Connor*.[32] There the driver of a bus had mounted a footpath and knocked down a girl but did not stop. The arresting garda saw the defendant drive the bus in an erratic manner: in turning off a dual carriageway it had swung very wide and swerved twice. On speaking to the defendant the garda noticed that his breath smelled of alcohol and that his speech was slurred. The defendant then failed an alcolyser test. The garda told the defendant that he was 'arresting him under section 49(6) of the 1961 Act for offences under section 49(2) and section 49(3)'. No evidence was given as to the formation of any opinion. It was held[33] by the Supreme Court that:

> when the garda said to the defendant that he was arresting him under section 49(6), he was by necessary implication invoking the terms of that section. When the words spoken are related to those terms and to the circumstances, the garda's evidence must be taken to mean that he had formed the opinion that the defendant had committed an offence under the section.

3.14   **The elements of a valid arrest**   A valid arrest[34] ordinarily entails two elements. It must, first, be conveyed to the person arrested that he is no longer at liberty. 'An arrest consists in or involves the seizure or touching of a person's body accompanied by a form of words which indicate to that person that he is under restraint. Whilst the older cases held that words alone would not suffice to constitute an arrest, nowadays words alone *may* amount to an arrest if, in the circumstances, they are calculated to bring, and do bring, to the person's notice that he was under restraint and he submitted to the compulsion. . . .'[35] Secondly, the person arrested should

---

31   At p. 46 of the report.
32   [1985] ILRM 333. See also *Director of Public Prosecutions v. Ó Súilleabháin*, unreported judgment of the High Court (Carroll J) delivered 5 May 1992.
33   At p. 335 of the report.
34   Here we are of course considering an arrest made without a warrant.
35   *Per* Hederman J in *Director of Public Prosecutions v. McCreesh* [1992] 2 IR 239, 250.

ordinarily be told why he is being deprived of his liberty. 'If a person is being asked by the law to submit to restraints upon his personal liberty, the law usually insists that he be acquainted in general terms with the reasons for such a restraint because only then is he in a position to decide whether or not it is appropriate to submit.'[36] In *Director of Public Prosecutions v. Mooney*[37] the defendant was stopped and breathalysed. The test proved positive and the garda formed the opinion that he had committed an offence under subsections 2 or 3 of section 49 as inserted by the 1978 Act (driving while the concentration of alcohol in the blood or urine exceeded the prescribed limit). The garda arrested the defendant under section 49(6) and informed him that this was for the offence of 'drunk driving'. In the garda station the defendant gave a urine specimen and the certificate subsequently issued by the Medical Bureau of Road Safety disclosed a concentration in excess of the permitted level. The defendant was charged with an offence under section 49(3), but in the District Court the charge was dismissed on the basis that the arrest was invalid: it was held by the District Judge that only an offence under section 49(1) (driving while under the influence of an intoxicant to such an extent as to be incapable of having proper control) could properly be described as 'drunk driving'. On appeal by way of case stated to the High Court it was, however, held that the arrest was not invalid and that the charge should not have been dismissed. Blayney J referred to the famous propositions laid down by Viscount Simon in *Christie v. Leachinsky*[38] and said[39] that:

> a garda in making an arrest does not have to use technical or precise language. Provided the arrested person knows in substance why he is being arrested the arrest is valid. So telling the respondent that he was being arrested for an offence of drunk driving was a sufficient communication of the reason for his arrest since in my opinion that could mean any of the three offences under the section. It told the respondent in substance why he was being arrested. Furthermore, . . . it must be doubtful if Garda Cloughley was required to give any reason at all. As the respondent had been required to blow into the breathalyser, and the results had been positive, the respondent must have been well aware of why he was being arrested.[40]

---

36 Ryan and Magee, *The Irish Criminal Process* (Dublin and Cork, 1983), p. 94.
37 [1992] 1 IR 548; [1993] ILRM 214.
38 [1947] AC 573, 587 and approved by O'Higgins CJ in *People (DPP) v. Walsh* [1980] IR 294, 306-307.
39 At pp. 553-554 of the report.
40 Blayney J's judgment is not without

3.15 If an arrest is not properly effected in the context of a drunken driving charge, the result may be an acquittal. The point is illustrated by *Director of Public Prosecutions v. Daly*[41] where the defendant was charged with an offence under section 49(3). The investigating garda had gone to the scene of a road traffic accident where he found a pedestrian lying unconscious at the side of the roadway. A few minutes later a car pulled up driven by the defendant who admitted he had been driving the car at the time of the accident. The garda formed the opinion that the defendant had consumed alcohol and he breathalysed him. The test proved positive and the defendant was arrested for drunken driving. The case stated records that: 'In cross-examination by Mr Gibbons the respondent's solicitor, Garda Clarke stated that the patrol car in which the alcolyzer was being kept was on the other side of the road from the respondent's car. The garda denied that he took the respondent by the arm to bring him to the patrol car but stated that he asked him to come across to the patrol car to the breath sampling equipment. The respondent gave evidence that following his admission of driving the car Garda Clarke took him by the arm and brought him to the squad car, Garda Clarke got in one door and the respondent in the other door. When asked if he felt he was under arrest the respondent stated "Well I couldn't leave let's put it like that; I was in his physical custody." In cross-examination the respondent stated that he believed he was under arrest and that he could not get away if he tried. He agreed that he did not try to get away. He agreed that the garda did not mention anything about an arrest to him until after the breath test.' The District Judge formed the opinion that the defendant had been deprived of his liberty when brought to the patrol car to be breathalysed

difficulty: at p. 551 of the report he expressed the view (obiter) that 'If, instead of telling the respondent that he was arresting him for 'an offence of drunk driving', (the garda) had told him he was arresting him for an offence under the section, there is no doubt that the arrest would have been perfectly valid. It probably would have been perfectly valid also if he had simply told the respondent that he was being arrested under s. 49, sub-s, 6 of the Act of 1961.' If the law is that the arrested person is entitled to know the reason for his arrest so as to enable him to decide whether he is obliged to submit, then it is submitted that it is not sufficient merely to cite to him section numbers of a Road Traffic Act.

41 Unwritten judgment of the High Court (Hamilton P, as he then was) delivered 3 March 1986. *Daly*, it should be noted, was decided under the provisions of the 1978 Act which did not, as does section 12(1) (b) of the 1994 Act, empower a garda to require a driver to 'accompany him to a place (including a vehicle) at or in the vicinity of (the) public place and there require him to provide . . . a specimen of his breath. . . .'

The Statutory Procedure: Part 1 39

and that, since he had not been informed of the reason for his arrest, the arrest was unlawful and the subsequent events were inadmissible in evidence. The President of the High Court held that the judge was correct in his decision to dismiss the charge.

3.16 What constitutes detention amounting to an arrest The decision in *Daly* points up a problem which is not unique to the sphere of drunken driving offences: to what extent may a garda detain a person before effecting an arrest?[42] 'In law,' it has been said,[43] 'there can be no half-way house between the liberty of the subject, unfettered by restraint, and an arrest.' So if a garda detains a person against his will, he must be in a position to justify that detention. He has, as we have seen, a common law power to stop vehicles and powers of arrest under sections 49 and 50 of the 1961 Act and section 12 of the 1994 Act.[44] In addition, the 1961 Act[45] creates an obligation on a driver to 'stop the vehicle on being so required by a member of the Garda Síochána and (to) keep it stationary for such period as is reasonably necessary in order to enable such member to discharge his duties'. The discharge of his duties would, one would expect, extend to reasonable inquiries necessary for the detection of crime and the apprehension of an offender. So, for example, in *People (DPP) v. McGinley*[46] it was decided that where a garda stopped a car at a checkpoint and the driver produced a Northern Ireland driving licence, he was entitled to examine and check the licence and to stop the vehicle while that was being done. But in that case the detention at the checkpoint lasted for over an hour as gardaí carried out security checks unrelated to the Road Traffic Acts. The court held[47] that this 'unnecessary detention at the checkpoint was tantamount to an arrest'.

3.17 Arrest at home or other private place Since the destination of a drunken driver is often his own home, it is not surprising that there have been cases concerning the validity of arrests effected by gardaí at, or in the vicinity of, a dwelling. These arrests have raised a particular problem because of the constitutional guarantee[48] that '(t)he dwelling of every citizen

---

42 In the case of drunken driving some answer is to be found in section 12(1)(b) and (c) of the 1994 Act; see para. 3.05 supra.
43 By Hanna J in *Dunne v. Clinton* [1930] IR 366, 372.
44 Paras. 3.04 and 3.10 supra.
45 Section 109(1) as amended by as amended by section 6 and the schedule to the 1968 Act.
46 Reported in *Judgments of the Court of Criminal Appeal 1984-1989*, edited by E. Casey, (Dublin, 1991), p. 233.
47 At p. 236 of the report.
48 In article 40, section 5 of Bunreacht na hÉireann, 1937.

is inviolable and shall not be forcibly entered save in accordance with law'. In the *Director of Public Prosecutions v. Gaffney*[49] it was alleged that the defendant had driven through a garda checkpoint. He was followed by gardaí and stopped in the driveway of his house. He refused, however, to remain there and continued into the house. The gardaí made two requests to enter which were refused by the defendant's brother who was then arrested for assault. On returning a third time to the front door the gardaí enquired if anyone was inside. A male voice answered: 'Yes, in here.' They entered the house and arrested the defendant. It was found as a fact in the District Court that there had been no invitation to the gardaí to enter. On a consultative case stated it was held by the High Court that the arrest was lawful; but on appeal to the Supreme Court it was held that the arrest constituted a violation of the constitutional guarantee of the inviolability of the dwelling. The case turned on the question whether the gardaí had permission to be in the dwelling and, on the facts, it was held they did not.

3.18 The Supreme Court did not in *Gaffney* overturn the earlier decision of the High Court in *Director of Public Prosecutions v. Closkey*[50] where an arrest in similar circumstances was upheld. In *Closkey* the defendant was again followed by gardaí to his home where they were admitted by his sister and found the defendant in bed apparently asleep. He was roused by one of the gardaí and arrested. His sister resisted and obstructed the arrest. It was argued by the defendant that her resistance was tantamount to a revocation of the permission given to the gardaí to enter the premises and that they were then bound to leave without effecting the arrest. But it was held that having lawfully entered the house, the gardaí were entitled to exercise their powers of arrest. The distinction between *Gaffney* and *Closkey* lies in the fact that in *Closkey* the gardaí had a licence to enter. But in *Gaffney* McCarthy J commented[51] as follows on *Closkey*: 'If the defendant's sister had, before the arrest, revoked the permission she had given, then Closkey's arrest would have been, in my view, unlawful. If O'Hanlon J held that, notwithstanding a prior revocation of permission by the defendant's sister, he was nonetheless lawfully arrested by the gardaí who had been lawfully admitted, in my view the case was incorrectly decided.'

49 [1987] IR 173. See O'Connor, 'The Validity of Arrests by the Garda Síochána whilst on Private Property', (1988) 6 ILT (NS) 254.

50 Unreported judgment of the High Court (O'Hanlon J) delivered 6 February 1984.

51 At p. 185 of the report.

3.19 The question of the validity of an arrest effected in a driveway leading to the dwelling was considered by the Supreme Court in *Director of Public Prosecutions v. McCreesh.*[52] Again gardaí had followed the defendant. When he reached the driveway of his own home, he got out of his car and headed for the door of the house. A garda approached him in the driveway and asked him his name which he gave. As a result of his observations of the defendant, the garda formed the opinion that he had committed an offence under section 49 and he told the defendant that he was arresting him. At that point the defendant told the garda that he was a trespasser and that he should leave. The garda then put his hand on the defendant's arm and arrested him. Arising out of these facts two questions were raised for the consideration of the Supreme Court: (1) whether a driveway forming part of the curtilage of a dwelling attracted the protection of article 40, section 5 of the Constitution and (2) if it did not, whether the gardaí were nevertheless trespassers on the occasion in question. In accordance with its usual practice the Supreme Court first considered the non-constitutional issue, and held that the gardaí were trespassers and that the arrest of the defendant was unlawful. According to Griffin J,[53] it follows from this decision that 'Under the law as at present in force (a garda's) power of arrest (under section 49) cannot be exercised if a driver succeeds in reaching his own premises, be they his private residence or his business premises, before the gardaí catch up with him.' McCarthy J commented:[54] It is clear, on the facts here, that at the time of the purported arrest, Garda Bolger was a trespasser; it may be that the Oireachtas may, by legislation, authorise an arrest without warrant in such circumstances; it has not done so. The relevant sections of the Act of 1978, including that substituting a new section 49 in the Act of 1961, clearly anticipate an offence committed in a public place and, possibly, also an arrest in such place. Whatever that case may be, if there is to be an arrest carried out in a private place by a garda who is a trespasser, such a mode of arrest requires express statutory provision in order to justify it at law.'

3.20 The defendant in *Director of Public Prosecutions v. Forbes*[55] relied on the judgment of McCarthy J in challenging his arrest. He had been stopped in his car. When gardaí in a patrol car approached, he drove off and was

---

52 [1992] 2 IR 239. See McDonagh, 'DPP v McCreesh — Case Note', (1991) 1 ICLJ 131. Although not expressly stated to do so, this decision must be taken to overrule that in *Director of Public Prosecutions v. Corrigan* [1986] IR 290; [1987] ILRM 575.
53 At p. 244 of the report.
54 At pp. 255-256 of the report.
55 [1994] 2 IR 542; [1993] ILRM 817.

followed by them. He stopped again in the driveway of a private house whereupon he got out the passenger's door of the car and ran for the road. He was caught by a garda who asked him where he was running to. 'Nowhere,' he replied. When asked did he live in the house the defendant said no and was unable to explain why he had driven into the driveway. Subsequently he was arrested for an offence under section 49 and the question arose as to the validity of his arrest: the defendant contended that it was invalid, as it had occurred on private property and not in a public place. O'Flaherty J, with whose judgment the other members of the court agreed, rejected this contention and held[56] that:

> Section 49, sub-s. 6 of the (1978) Act provides that a member of the Garda Síochána may arrest without warrant a person who in the member's opinion is committing *or has committed* an offence under the section. The offence, of course, must be committed in a public place but provided the garda does not breach any constitutional or legal right of another, he is entitled to go on other property to effect an arrest. Here there is no question that the gardaí were trespassers. It must be regarded as axiomatic that any householder gives an implied authority to a member of the garda to come onto the forecourt of his premises to see to the enforcement of the law or prevent a breach thereof. It will be clear that this case is not concerned with any question of entering a dwelling-house and, therefore, there is not in the instant case any question of any form of implied waiver of any constitutional right. Further, like any implied authority, it is an implication which the evidence may, on occasion, rebut. Clearly, in this case, the gardaí were acting in the execution of their duties. They saw a car which was driven suspiciously, to say the least; it went up a side road and into the driveway of a private dwelling. Could it be said what danger the driver of such a car might have posed for the occupants of that dwellinghouse? In the circumstances of this case, the gardaí were clearly acting in the execution of their duties. This must be the acid test because they cannot be regarded as acting in the execution of their duties if they breach anyone's constitutional or legal rights (unless in an extreme situation, such as in the defence of life or limb). For them to have ignored the defendant's conduct on this occasion would have bordered on a dereliction of duty on their part. To suggest that they would be perfectly entitled to arrest the defendant if he was on the public road but not if he was on a third

---

56 At p. 548 of the report.

The Statutory Procedure: Part 1 43

party's property would constitute, as was suggested in the course of the debate before us, a massive absurdity.

3.21 The foregoing decisions preceded the enactment of the 1994 Act which differs from its predecessor in that the scope of a garda's power of arrest under sections 49 and 50 has been widened: he is now authorised[57] 'for the purpose arresting a person under section 49(8) or 50(10) of the (1961) Act (to) enter without warrant (if need be by use of reasonable force) any place (including the curtilage of a dwelling but not including a dwelling) where the person is or where the member, with reasonable cause, suspects him to be'. The purpose of these words is to change the status of a garda who enters a place other than a dwelling, without permission or contrary to the terms of a permission, in order to effect an arrest under one of the sections: he is no longer a trespasser for he enters under a lawful excuse. Thus if the facts of the *McCreesh*[58] case were to recur, the arrest of the defendant, in such circumstances, could not now be challenged.

3.22 **The procedure following arrest** Ordinarily an arrest is, as Walsh J described in *People v. Shaw*,[59] 'simply a process of ensuring the attendance at Court of the person arrested'. In the context of a drunken driving prosecution an arrest is something more than that: it is a step which must be taken before a requirement may be made of a defendant under section 13 of the 1994 Act that he furnish either two specimens of breath by exhaling into an apparatus for determining the concentration alcohol in the breath or a blood or urine specimen to a designated doctor for analysis by the Medical Bureau of Road Safety. This follows from the words of section 13 which state that the requirement that a person furnish a specimen may be made at a Garda Síochána station '(w)here a person is arrested under section 49(8) or section 50(10) of the Principal Act or section 12(3), or where a person is arrested under section 53(6) (for dangerous driving), 106(3A) (for failing to stop at or leaving the scene of a traffic accident resulting in injury) or 112(6) (for unauthorised taking of a mechanically propelled vehicle) of the Principal Act and a member of the Garda Síochána is of opinion that the person has consumed an intoxicant. . . .' Following his arrest a defendant should therefore be brought to a garda station. If he goes voluntarily without having been arrested, it was held[60] that, under the provisions of the 1978 Act, there was no power to require him to provide a specimen. But where there has been an arrest and the defendant

57 By section 39(2).
58 Supra.
59 [1982] IR 1, 29.

60 *People (DPP) v. Greeley* [1985] ILRM 320; see para. 3.10 supra.

has been brought to a garda station, he may, if necessary for the purpose of obtaining a specimen, be brought to a second garda station.[61]

3.23 The arrest upon an arrest Suppose a person has been arrested for an offence unrelated to drunken driving, and the garda then decides to initiate steps to prosecute him for a drunken driving offence. The question arises in these circumstances whether the defendant should first be released from custody in respect of the offence for which he has already been arrested and then rearrested for the drunken driving offence. As a rule the law favours the view that there cannot be an arrest upon an arrest.[62] Thus in *State (Walsh) v. Maguire*[63] the defendant had been arrested under section 30 of the Offences Against the State Act 1939. He was brought to a garda station where he was detained and some time later was arrested again. Commenting on the second arrest, Henchy J held[64] that: 'As an arrest means a physical act done with a view to detention, and since the accused was already arrested and in detention, this cannot have been an arrest in law.'[65]

DISPOSITION OF THE VEHICLE

3.24 Where a member of the Garda Síochána has, under the Road Traffic Acts 1961 to 1994, arrested without warrant a person in charge of a mechanically propelled vehicle, he is empowered, if the circumstances require, to take such steps as he may consider proper for the temporary disposition of the vehicle.[66] The compulsory insurance requirements of the Road Traffic Act 1961 do not apply to a garda using a vehicle for the purpose of so disposing of it.[67] Further powers of detention are provided for in the Road Traffic Act 1994[68] which enables the Minister for the

---

61 *Director of Public Prosecutions v. Sheehy* [1987] ILRM 138.
62 See *State (Hoey) v. Garvey* [1978] IR 1, 4 per Finlay P (as he then was): '... the position at common law was that in the ordinary way a person suspected of being involved in the commission of any crime could be arrested by a member of the Garda Síochána and, if and when so arrested, his position was that he could either be released as soon as may be if the suspicion proved immediately groundless; and that if not, he must be charged as soon as may be'.
63 [1979] IR 372.
64 At p. 386 of the report.
65 Cf. *People (DPP) v. Shaw* [1982] IR 1 and *People (DPP) v. Kehoe* [1985] IR 444; [1986] ILRM 690.
66 Section 110 of the Road Traffic Act 1961 as amended by section 49(1)(k) of the Road Traffic Act 1994.
67 Section 4(2) of the Road Traffic Act 1961.
68 Section 41.

Environment, after consultation with the Minister for Justice, to make regulations 'authorising and providing for the detention, removal, storage and subsequent release or disposal of a mechanically propelled vehicle in use in a public place' where the driver has refused or failed to produce a driving licence and the garda is of opinion that he is too young to hold a licence, where the garda is of opinion that the vehicle is being used in contravention of the compulsory insurance requirements of the 1961 Act, or where the garda is of opinion that excise duty payable in respect of the vehicle has not been paid for a continuous period of three months or more prior to its use. These regulations have now been made: see the Road Traffic Act 1994 (Section 41) Regulations, 1995.[69]

---

[69] SI No. 89 of 1995

4

The Statutory Procedure in Drunken Driving Cases: Part 2

TREATMENT OF THE DEFENDANT IN THE GARDA STATION

4.01 The Criminal Justice Act 1984 (Treatment of Persons in Custody in Garda Síochána Stations) Regulations, 1987[1] regulate the treatment of persons in custody in garda stations. In the context of a person arrested for a drunken driving offence, the following provisions of the regulations are noteworthy. A record (known as a custody record) must be kept in respect of the person in which must be recorded such information as is required to be recorded by the regulations.[2] The member in charge of the garda station must inform him, or cause him to be informed, (1) in ordinary language of the offence in respect of which he has been arrested, (2) that he is entitled to consult a solicitor, and (3) that he is entitled to have notification of his being in custody in the station sent to another person.[3] A written notice informing the person of his rights must be given to him and he must be asked to sign the custody record in acknowledgment of receipt of the notice.[4] If the arrested person has asked for a solicitor, or has asked that a person reasonably named by him should be notified of his being in custody, the member in charge of the station must notify or cause to be notified the solicitor or person as soon as practicable.[5] If the solicitor or named person cannot be contacted within a reasonable time or if the solicitor is unable or unwilling to attend at the station, the person must be given an opportunity to ask for another solicitor or that another person reasonably named by him should be notified.[6] If he asks for another solicitor

---

1 SI No. 119 of 1987.
2 Criminal Justice Act 1984 (Treatment of Persons in Custody in Garda Síochána Stations) Regulations, 1987 article 6(1) and (2). A copy of the custody record must be supplied to the arrested person or his legal representative on request made within 12 months after he ceases to be in custody: ibid., article 24(2).
3 Ibid., article 8(1).
4 Ibid., article 8(2) and (4).
5 Ibid., article 9(2)(a)(i).
6 Ibid., article 9(2)(a)(ii).

or that another person be notified, the member in charge again must notify or cause to be notified the other solicitor or person as soon as practicable.[7] The arrested person is entitled to reasonable access to the solicitor of his choice and to be enabled to communicate with him privately.[8] Under the Criminal Justice Act 1984[9] it is provided that a breach of the regulations, although it may render a member of the Garda Síochána liable to disciplinary proceedings, does not of itself affect the lawfulness of the custody of the detained person. In *Director of Public Prosecutions v. Spratt*[10] the High Court considered whether the absence of evidence that the regulations had been complied with invalidated a prosecution for a drunken driving offence. O'Hanlon J held that although the prosecution must prove that the regulations were complied with, a failure to offer such proof, or indeed non-compliance with the regulations, does not of itself invalidate the prosecution: the matter is one of judicial discretion to be exercised having regard to all the circumstances of the case.

THE DEFENDANT'S RIGHT OF ACCESS TO A SOLICITOR WHILE IN THE GARDA STATION

4.02 A defendant's right of access to a solicitor while in custody was outlined in *People v. Madden*[11] where it was said that: 'This Court is satisfied that a person held in detention by the Garda Síochána, whether under the provisions of the (Offences Against the State) Act of 1939 or otherwise, has got a right of reasonable access to his legal advisers and that a refusal of a request to give such reasonable access would render his detention illegal. Of course, in this context the word "reasonable" must be construed having regard to all the circumstances of each individual case and, in particular, as to the time at which access is requested and the availability of the legal adviser or advisers sought. However, the court is not satisfied that there is any obligation on the Garda Síochána when detaining a person either under section 30 of the Act of 1939 or under any other authority, to proffer to such person the assistance of a legal adviser

---

7 Ibid.
8 Ibid., article 11(1).
9 Section 7(3) and (4).
10 Unreported judgment of the High Court (O'Hanlon J) delivered 8 February 1995.
11 [1977] IR 336, 355. See also *In re Emergency Powers Bill, 1976* [1977] IR 159; *People (DPP) v. Farrell* [1978] IR 13; *People (DPP) v. Pringle* (1981) 2 Frewen 57; *People (DPP) v. Shaw* [1982] IR 1; and *People (DPP) v. Conroy* [1986] IR 460; [1988] ILRM 4. The right is a constitutional right and not merely a legal one: *People (DPP) v. Healy* [1990] 2 IR 73; [1990] ILRM 313.

without request.' This right of access was invoked by the defendant in *Walsh v. Ó Buachalla*.[12] Having been arrested for drunken driving and brought to Dun Laoghaire garda station, he was put into the parade room and given a document entitled 'Information for Persons in Custody' which under the heading 'Legal Advice' stated: 'You may communicate privately with a solicitor either in writing or by telephone or consult with the solicitor in the station.' The arresting garda advised the defendant to read the document which he did. A doctor was summoned, but there was a delay of nearly an hour until he arrived to attend on the defendant. Having introduced the doctor to the defendant, the garda required the defendant to produce a specimen. At that stage the defendant said he wanted a solicitor. The garda told him it was too late to make the request; that he had had the opportunity to contact a solicitor while waiting in the parade room which had a telephone in it. He told the defendant he could, if he wished, contact a solicitor once the specimen had been taken. The defendant gave a blood specimen, which on analysis was found to have a concentration of 192 milligrammes of alcohol per 100 millilitres of blood, but did not afterwards seek to contact a solicitor from the garda station. On the defendant's application for judicial review it was submitted that his constitutional right of access to a solicitor had been infringed by the garda's refusal to accede to his request and that the evidence subsequently obtained, i.e. the specimen of blood which formed the subject-matter of the bureau's certificate, was rendered inadmissible. Rejecting this submission, Blayney J thought it was 'doubtful' that there had been any violation of the defendant's constitutional rights and, on the assumption that there had been a violation, he held[13] that 'the evidence here was not obtained as a result of the violation of the applicant's constitutional rights. It is a case of "post hoc sed non propter hoc"—the evidence was obtained after the violation but not as a result of the violation. The applicant was obliged by statute to give a specimen of his blood or urine. No advice from a solicitor could have altered that. So his being refused access to a solicitor did not in any way lead to the specimen of blood being obtained. Either that specimen or a specimen of the applicant's urine would have been obtained anyway because Garda Fahy was entitled to require the applicant to provide them.'

4.03 The judgment of Blayney J in *Walsh v. Ó Buachalla* comes perilously close to saying that because the defendant had an obligation to provide a specimen, a failure to afford him his constitutional right was irrelevant. It

12 [1991] 1 IR 56.   13 At pp. 59-60 of the report.

certainly does imply that the only evidence which can be excluded because of a breach of a constitutional right is evidence obtained by and on account of that breach. But this may not be the law. In at least one case in the District Court there has been evidence that a defendant, who was charged with a refusal under section 13 of the 1978 Act, had in fact refused because of the failure by the gardaí to comply with his request to be allowed contact his solicitor.[14] In these circumstances the District Judge acquitted. His decision may be viewed as one of those cases referred to by McCarthy J, speaking in a different context,[15] 'in which a District Justice in pursuance of his constitutional duty, having regard to some outrage committed upon a person brought before a District Court, would refuse to proceed. . . .'

THE OBLIGATION TO PROVIDE A SPECIMEN AT THE GARDA STATION

4.04 Section 13 of the 1994 Act obliges arrested persons to furnish specimens in accordance with the requirements of a member of the Garda Síochána and a designated doctor. Where a person has been arrested under section 49(8) of the 1961 Act, section 50(10) of the 1961 Act or section 12(3) of the 1994 Act, or where a person has been arrested under section 53(6) of the 1961 Act (for dangerous driving), section 106(3A) of the 1961 Act (for leaving the scene of a road traffic accident involving injury to the person) or section 112(6) of the 1961 Act (for unauthorised taking of a mechanically propelled vehicle) and a member of the Garda Síochána is of opinion that he has consumed an intoxicant, a member of the Garda Síochána may at his discretion take the following steps while the person is in a garda station. He may require the person either to permit a designated doctor to take from him a specimen of his blood or, at the option of the person, to provide for the designated doctor a specimen of his urine.[16] If the doctor states in writing that he is unwilling, on medical grounds, to take from the person or be provided by him with the specimen to which the requirement related, the garda may require the person to furnish a specimen other than that to which the first requirement related.[17] A person who, following a requirement, refuses or fails to comply with it, or refuses or fails to comply with a requirement of a designated doctor in relation to the taking of a blood specimen or the provision of a urine specimen, is guilty of an offence.[18] The garda is also empowered to require

---

14 *Director of Public Prosecutions v. Byrne*, 'Meath Chronicle', 1 June 1991.
15 In *Keating v. The Governor of Mountjoy Prison* [1991] 1 IR 61, 65; [1990] ILRM 850.
16 Section 13(1)(b) of the 1994 Act.
17 Ibid.
18 Section 13(3) of the 1994 Act; see

the person to provide two specimens of his breath by exhaling into an apparatus for indicating the concentration of alcohol in the breath.[19] This procedure is not, as yet, used in practice.

4.05 The requirement The requirement that a person furnish a blood or urine specimen will, as we have seen, be made under section 13 of the 1994 Act. Under the 1978 Act a requirement could have been made under either section 13 or section 14 of that Act depending on whether a person had been arrested under section 49 for drunken driving or section 50 for being drunk in charge. Although the requirement of the person under both sections was essentially the same, ie, that he either permit a designated registered medical practitioner to take from him a specimen of his blood or, at his option, provide for a designated registered medical practitioner a specimen of his urine, it was held by the Supreme Court that, where a person was charged under one of the sections, the prosecution must prove under which of the sections the requirement had been made.[20] Although the justification is not as strong under the 1994 Act, since there is no alternative section under which a similar requirement could be made, a garda should still expressly invoke section 13(1)(b) when he makes his requirement, and he should explain to the person the consequences of a failure or refusal to comply. But if the person furnishes a specimen and is then prosecuted for an offence under section 49, it is not necessary for the prosecution to prove that the consequences of a failure or refusal were first explained to him.[21]

4.06 The obligations In practice, following an arrest under section 49, a garda will make a requirement under section 13(1)(b) that the person either permit a designated doctor to take from him a specimen of his blood or, at the option of the person, provide for the designated doctor a specimen of his urine. If the person avails of the option and chooses to provide urine but finds that he is unable to do so, he is not guilty of an offence; in such circumstances the obligation to permit the taking of a blood specimen revives, and should he then fail or refuse to permit that specimen to be

paras 4.05-4.07 infra. Where a person is prosecuted for refusal or failure to comply with a requirement it is not necessary to prove the time of driving or attempting to drive: *Director of Public Prosecutions v. Clinton* [1984] ILRM 127.

19 Section 13(1)(a) of the 1994 Act; see paras. 4.22-4.23 infra.

20 *Director of Public Prosecutions v. McGarrigle*, unreported decision of the Supreme Court, judgment delivered 22 June 1987.

21 *Director of Public Prosecutions v. Hand* [1994] 1 IR 577.

taken, that is the offence with which he should be charged.[22] Once the garda has made his requirement, there is a further obligation to comply with a requirement of the designated doctor in relation to the taking or provision of the specimen.[23] This obligation 'is concerned with ensuring that the defendant will comply with any instructions which the doctor may give him in relation to taking a specimen of his blood or getting him to provide a specimen of his urine. For example, in relation to taking a specimen of his blood, the doctor might need to require a defendant to take off his coat and roll up the sleeve of his shirt so that he could take blood from a vein in his arm. And in relation to providing a specimen of urine, the doctor might require the defendant to provide a particular quantity of urine or to provide it in a particular receptacle or provide the specimen to the doctor in his presence or make some other necessary requirement.'[24]

4.07 Refusal or failure for a special and substantial reason In a prosecution for an offence alleging a refusal or failure to permit a designated doctor to take a specimen of blood or for refusal or failure to comply with a requirement of a designated doctor in relation to the taking of a specimen of blood, it is a defence for the defendant to satisfy the court that there was a special and substantial reason for his refusal or failure and that, as soon as practicable after the refusal or failure, he complied (or offered, but was not called upon, to comply) with a requirement in relation to the provision of a specimen of urine.[25] The only Irish authority as to the meaning of a 'special and substantial' reason is *Gallagher v. O'Hanlon*,[26] a case decided under the provisions of the Road Traffic Act 1968, where it was argued on behalf of the defendant that on a charge of refusing or failing to furnish a blood specimen evidence should be given to establish the time of driving, since furnishing a specimen outside the period of three hours from the time of driving would serve no purpose. For the prosecution it was argued that the relevant section (section 30 of the 1968 Act,

---

22 *Director of Public Prosecutions (Coughlan) v. Swan* [1994] 1 ILRM 314.
23 Section 13(3) of the 1994 Act.
24 Per Blayney J in *Director of Public Prosecutions (Coughlan) v. Swan*, supra, at p. 320 of the report.
25 Section 23(2) of the 1994 Act. Notwithstanding that the Act allows for this defence, evidence may be given at the hearing of a charge for an offence under section 49 or 50 that the defendant refused or failed to comply with a requirement to permit the taking of a blood specimen or to comply with a requirement of a designated doctor in relation to the taking of a blood specimen: section 23(3) of the 1994 Act.
26 Unreported judgment of the High Court (Finlay P, as he then was) delivered 10 July 1975.

corresponding to section 13 of the 1994 Act) did not contain any requirement that proof be given of the time of driving and, furthermore, if a requirement were made outside the period of three hours there would be a special and substantial reason for refusing or failing to furnish the specimen. Finlay P accepted both prosecution arguments. 'I have no doubt,' he said,[27] 'that a Court, before whom a person appeared who had refused to comply with the request under section 30 if they were satisfied upon proof by the defendant that the request was made more than three hours after the driving, would be entitled and almost bound to accept that as a special and substantial reason for declining the request.' The corresponding statutory provision in England makes it a defence to failing to provide a specimen for the defendant to show that he had 'reasonable excuse'. The excuse must, however, be related to the capacity of the person to supply the sample; so in *R. v. John*[28] it was held that religious beliefs which precluded the defendant from giving a sample did not amount to a reasonable excuse. For mental condition or physical injuries to constitute a reasonable excuse they must, it was said in *Rowland v. Thorpe*,[29] be of a very extreme character. But it was accepted in *R. v. Knightley*[30] that confusion caused by concussion might be a reasonable excuse. In *Director of Public Prosecution v. Fountain*,[31] on being required to provide a blood specimen, the defendant said: 'In view of the danger of Aids I would rather not give blood.' The defendant's belief that the provision of a blood specimen thus posed a risk of injury to his health did not, it was held, constitute a reasonable excuse.

4.08 The obligation to provide a specimen while in hospital One of the innovations in the 1994 Act is the conferral on a member of the Garda Síochána of power to require a person, while in hospital, to permit a designated doctor to take from him a blood specimen or, at his option, to provide for the designated doctor a urine specimen.[32] The power arises where an event has occurred in a public place in relation to a mechanically propelled vehicle in consequence of which the person is injured, or claims

---

27 At p. 7 of the judgment.
28 [1974] 1 WLR 624; [1974] 2 All ER 561; [1974] RTR 332.
29 [1970] 3 All ER 195; [1970] RTR 406.
30 [1971] 1 WLR 1073; [1971] 2 All ER 1041; [1971] RTR 409.
31 [1988] RTR 385.
32 For this purpose a garda is empowered to enter without warrant any hospital where the person is or where the garda, with reasonable cause, suspects him to be: section 39(3) of the 1994 Act. So too a designated doctor is empowered to enter a hospital for the purpose of taking a specimen of blood or being provided with a specimen of urine: section 39(4) of the 1994 Act.

The Statutory Procedure: Part 2

or appears to have been injured, and is admitted to, or attends at, a hospital.[33] Before making his requirement the garda must be of opinion that the person, at the time of the event, was driving or attempting to drive, or in charge of with intent to drive or attempt to drive, the mechanically propelled vehicle and that he had consumed an intoxicant.[34] But if, the garda having made the requirement of a blood or urine specimen, the doctor states in writing that he is unwilling, on medical grounds, to take from the person or be provided by him with the specimen to which the requirement related, the garda may then make a requirement of the person in relation to the specimen other than that to which the first requirement related.[35]

4.09 Refusal or failure to comply with the requirement made in hospital, or to comply with a requirement of a designated doctor in relation to the taking of a specimen of blood or the provision of a specimen of urine, is an offence.[36] But in a prosecution for refusing or failing to comply with a requirement to permit the taking of a blood specimen or for refusing or failing to comply with a requirement of a designated doctor in relation to the taking of such a specimen, it is a defence to show that there was a 'special and substantial' reason for the refusal or failure and that the defendant complied (or offered, but was not called upon, to comply) with a requirement in relation to the provision of a specimen of urine.[37] It is also a defence for a person charged with an offence of refusing or failing under section 15 to show that following his admission to, or attendance at, a hospital he came under the care of a doctor and the doctor refused, on medical grounds, to permit the taking or provision of the specimen concerned.[38]

PROCEDURE AT THE GARDA STATION REGARDING SPECIMENS

4.10 Division of the specimen and completion of the doctor's form
Where a designated doctor has taken a blood specimen or has been provided with a urine specimen, he must divide the specimen into two parts and place each part in a container which he must seal forthwith.[39] He must

---

33 Section 15(1) of the 1994 Act.
34 Ibid.
35 Ibid.
36 Section 15(2) of the 1994 Act.
37 Section 15(2) and section 23(2) of the 1994 Act; see para. 4.07 supra.
38 Section 15(3) of the 1994 Act.

39 Section 18(1) of the 1994 Act. It is not necessary for the prosecution to prove that the doctor had used any particular equipment for the purpose of taking the specimen or that the equipment used had been provided by the bureau: *State (Quinn) v. Connellan*, unre-

also complete the prescribed form.[40] The manner of completion by a doctor of this form was considered by the Supreme Court in *Director of Public Prosecutions v. Collins*.[41] The doctor had affixed his signature to the last line of the form, but had left blank the line in the form after the words 'I, the undersigned designated registered medical practitioner' where it was evidently intended that he should insert his name.[42] The Supreme Court rejected the submission that the doctor had not duly completed the form. It was pointed out by Henchy J[43] that if the doctor had inserted his name in the blank line:

> the form would have *looked* more complete, but the insertion would have made only a visual difference. What was required to complete (i.e. to make whole) this part of the form was for the designated medical practitioner to verify, by signing his name at the end line, that he had done the several things recited in the printed form as having been done by him. The opening words 'I, the undersigned designated registered medical practitioner' and the signature at the end identify one and the same person, and the signature purports to aver that (the doctor) did the acts which the intervening part of the form attributes to him.

The form was also attacked because of the doctor's failure to delete in full the line referring to a specimen of urine. He had failed to delete the whole of the phrase 'obtained from the person named at 1 *above the specimen of his urine*'. He had deleted only the words italicised. The Supreme Court held that the failure to delete all the words was 'obviously a slip' and the fact that the doctor drew a line through the italicised words 'would prevent any reader of the signed form from realistically concluding that it was other than a completed form in respect of the blood sample in question'.

4.11 In the *Director of Public Prosecutions v. O'Neill*[44] the defendant challenged the completion of the doctor's form because it referred to the time of provision of the specimen as 12.50 without indicating whether it had been provided during the day or at night. The Supreme Court rejected the submission because the time at which the sample was furnished had

ported judgment of the High Court (Egan J) delivered 9 July 1984.
40 Ibid.
41 [1981] ILRM 447.
42 See appendix C for the lay-out of the form.
43 At p. 449 of the report.
44 Unreported decision of the Supreme Court, judgment of Hederman J delivered 30 July 1984.

been established by other evidence and the defendant could not have been under any misapprehension as to the precise time nor could he have been prejudiced by the omission to state whether the time was a.m. or p.m.

4.12 The offer of the container to the defendant and the forwarding of the container and doctor's form to the bureau After the specimen has been divided into two parts, a member of the Garda Síochána must offer one of the sealed containers to the person from whom it has been obtained together with a statement in writing that he may retain either of the containers.[45] As soon as practicable after that, a member of the Garda Síochána must cause the doctor's completed form, together with the relevant sealed container, or, where the person has declined to retain one of the containers, both sealed containers to be forwarded to the bureau.[46] There is a rebuttable presumption that the foregoing requirements have been complied with.[47] In *Director of Public Prosecutions v. Byrne*[48] the evidence disclosed that there had been a delay of a number of days before the garda forwarded the container and doctor's form to the bureau. The Supreme Court rejected the defendant's contention that the garda had failed to comply with his obligation to forward the items 'as soon as practicable'. The court relied on the fact that no evidence had been adduced by or on behalf of the defendant to show that it would have been practicable to forward the items sooner than they were in fact forwarded, and held that the delay did not of itself discharge the presumption that the statutory requirement had been met.

4.13 The practice of sending a duplicate of the doctor's form to the bureau was challenged in *Director of Public Prosecutions v. Kemmy*[49] as not being in compliance with the 1978 Act. It was established that the medical practitioner had completed and signed duplicate forms, one of which lay exactly underneath the other, and that the forms were so made that, as he wrote each entry and his signature on the upper form, the same entries and signature were written by him on the corresponding parts of the lower form. Only the lower duplicate form was sent to the bureau with the relevant container. A majority of the Supreme Court held that the form sent to the bureau was the duly completed form required by the statute.

---

45 Section 18(2) of the 1994 Act.
46 Section 18(3) of the 1994 Act.
47 As there is that the doctor has divided the specimen into two parts, placed each in a sealed container and completed the prescribed form: section 18(4) of the 1994 Act.
48 Unwritten decision of the Supreme Court, judgment delivered 21 March 1984.
49 [1980] IR 160.

DETENTION OF INTOXICATED DRIVERS

4.14 The 1994 Act (section 16) confers a new power on the member of the Garda Síochána in charge of a garda station to detain in custody a person arrested for drunken driving, or certain related offences, if 'of opinion that the person is under the influence of an intoxicant to such an extent as to be a threat to the safety of himself or others'.[50] The person may be detained for such period, not exceeding six hours from the time of arrest, as the member in charge of the station considers necessary.[51] It is clear from the terms of the section that this power may be used only to protect the safety of the person and others: it is not a form of punishment.

4.15 Where a person is detained under section 16, the member in charge of the station must, if the person is over 18 years of age or the member is of opinion that he is over 18, as soon as is practicable, if it is reasonably possible to do so, inform a relative of the person or such other person as the person detained may specify of the detention, unless the person does not wish anybody to be so informed.[52] He must do the same if the person detained is under 18 or the member is of opinion that he is under 18; the detainee under 18 cannot waive the requirement that another person be informed of his detention.[53] Upon the attendance of the relative or other specified person at the station, the detainee over 18 must be released into his custody unless he himself is under 18 or the member in charge of the station is of opinion that he is under 18, or the detainee does not wish to be released into his custody, or the member is of the opinion that the detainee continues to be under the influence of an intoxicant to such an extent that, if he is released into the custody of the relative or other person, he will continue to be a threat to the safety of himself or others.[54] If he is not released into the custody of the relative or other specified person, the detainee must be still be released at the expiration of the period of six hours from the time of arrest.[55] The detainee under 18, or who the member is of opinion is under 18, must be released into the custody of a relative or specified person who attends at the garda station, unless the latter is under 18 or the member is of opinion that he is under 18.[56] If not so released, the detainee under 18 must also be released at the expiration of six hours.[57]

---

50 Section 16(1) of the 1994 Act.
51 Ibid.
52 Section 16(2) of the 1994 Act.
53 Ibid.
54 Section 16(3)(a) of the 1994 Act.
55 Ibid.
56 Section 16(3)(b) of the 1994 Act.
57 Ibid.

PROCEDURE AT THE BUREAU REGARDING SPECIMENS

4.16 The bureau must analyse the specimen and determine the concentration of alcohol in it as soon as practicable after it has been received.[58] Where the bureau receives two specimens of blood or two specimens of urine taken from the same person, it is sufficient for it to make an analysis and determination in relation to one of the two specimens.[59] As soon as practicable after the analysis and determination have been made, the bureau must forward a completed certificate in the prescribed form to the garda station from which the specimen analysed was forwarded.[60] It must also, as soon as practicable, forward a copy of the completed certificate to the person who is named in the doctor's form as the person from whom the specimen was taken or who provided it.[61] There is a rebuttable presumption that the foregoing requirements have been complied with and it is, furthermore, provided that the certificate is evidence of compliance by the bureau with the requirements placed on it.[62]

4.17 The performance of duties as soon as practicable The question whether the bureau performed its duties 'as soon as practicable' has been raised on a number of occasions. In *Hobbs v. Hurley*[63] the High Court considered whether the bureau had in that case forwarded its certificate 'as soon as practicable'. Costello J (as he then was) laid down three propositions having regard to the decided cases:[64]

> Firstly, the statute requires the Bureau to forward the certificate 'as soon as practicable' after the specimen has been analysed and the concentration of alcohol in it has been determined. These words are not synonymous with an obligation to forward it 'as soon as possible'. Had such words been used, they would have imposed a more severe obligation on the Bureau than it now in fact has. Secondly, it must be borne in mind that the obligation imposed by the section is contained in a penal statute and so must be strictly construed. Thirdly, when considering what difficulties can properly be taken into account in deciding whether the Bureau's statutory obligation was carried out 'as soon as practicable' the content and surrounding

---

58 Section 19(1) of the 1994 Act.
59 Section 19(2) of the 1994 Act.
60 Section 19(3) of the 1994 Act.
61 Ibid.
62 Section 19(4) and section 21(3) of the 1994 Act and see paras. 5.02 et seq.

post.
63 Unreported judgment of the High Court (Costello J, as he then was) delivered 10 June 1980.
64 At p. 12 of the judgment.

circumstances should be considered. In particular the nature and purpose of the obligation must be borne in mind.

Applying these principles to the obligations of the bureau under section 22(3) of the 1978 Act which corresponds to section 19(3) of the 1994 Act, Costello J held that:[65]

> The completed certificate is required to be sent to the Garda Station 'as soon as practicable' because the prosecuting authorities will need it to decide under which sub-section (if any) of section 49 the arrested person should be prosecuted. The arrested person may himself have retained a specimen of blood or urine for analysis . . . and it is clear that the purpose of sending him a copy of the certificate 'as soon as practicable' is to make him aware of the evidence which may be adduced against him and to afford him an adequate opportunity to prepare his defence should the certificate be adverse to him.

On the facts of the case the judge held[66] that upon the bureau

> forwarding the documents twenty days after the determination of the alcohol concentration in the specimen the prosecuting authorities were given ample time in which to consider the nature of the evidence against the defendant and the defendant was afforded ample time in which to prepare his defence. If, then, the Bureau fulfilled the purpose of the statutory obligation imposed on it by the section by sending the documents on the day they did, the court can take into account those practical difficulties which prevented the Bureau forwarding the documents at an earlier date. In doing so I can conclude that it was not feasible for the Bureau to carry out its duties sooner than it did, that it forwarded the documents as soon as was practicable in all the circumstances of the case and that it was not in breach of its statutory duties.

4.18 The same point arose in *Director of Public Prosecutions v. Corrigan*[67] where it was argued that the bureau had not only failed to forward the certificate, but had failed to carry out its analysis as soon as practicable. The defendant had been arrested on 24 October 1979 and gave a sample

---

65 At pp. 14-15 of the judgment.
66 At pp. 15-16 of the judgment.
67 Unreported judgment of the High Court (Finlay P, as he then was) delivered 21 July 1980.

of his blood which was sent on the same date to the bureau. The bureau's certificate was dated 13 November 1979 and the seal was fixed on 15 November 1979. The garda's evidence was that he received the certificate from the bureau at some time before 18 December 1979. Finlay P (as he then was), following the decision in *Hobbs v. Hurley*,[68] said that:

> Having regard to the presumption contained in section 23 (section 21 of the 1994 Act) it seems to me clear that it is not possible from a mere lapse of time without any other evidence, and it certainly would not be possible from a lapse of time of approximately a month without any other evidence, for a Court properly to reach the conclusion that a specimen was either not analysed or a certificate was not sent as soon as practicable. In order for the Court to reach a decision to that effect it would be necessary for it to have before it material indicating the practical difficulties and surrounding circumstances under which either or both of these activities was carried out by the Bureau on the one hand and the effect and consequence of any delay that occurred on the other. The onus of establishing the facts from which a Court could draw conclusions on these two topics is clearly, having regard to the terms of the Sections, upon the Defendant.[69]

He went on:[70]

> In the instant case therefore where no evidence was apparently adduced by the Defendant with regard to the practical difficulties or factors surrounding any delay that occurred within the administration of the Bureau and where apparently the Defendant did not even adduce evidence of the date upon which he received a copy of the Certificate and certainly adduced no evidence to indicate that that date left him in any way prejudiced or that the purpose of his receiving it as soon as practicable was defeated by delay, it does not seem to me that the learned District Justice was entitled to reach a conclusion as he apparently did that either the specimen had not been analysed as soon as practicable or that the certificate had not been sent as soon as practicable.

---

68 Supra.
69 At pp. 8-9 of the judgment. This passage was expressly approved by Henchy J in the Supreme Court in *Director of Public Prosecutions v. Collins* [1981] ILRM 447.
70 At pp. 9-10 of the judgment.

The decision in *Director of Public Prosecutions v. Corrigan* was applied in *Director of Public Prosecutions v. Spaight*.[71] Here the specimen had been posted to the bureau on 6 December 1978; the analysis was completed on 19 December 1978; and the certificate was posted to the defendant and the garda station on 12 January 1979. It was not received in the garda station until 5 February 1979. The defendant's argument that the certificate and the copy had not been forwarded as soon as practicable after completion of the analysis was rejected. Finlay P (as he then was) pointed out that:[72]

> No evidence was given of the practical difficulties and surrounding circumstances under which the activity of issuing a certificate was carried out by the Bureau nor was any evidence given of the effect or consequence of any delay that occurred. Evidence ... that in other cases on other occasions a certificate was issued in a shorter time than in the instant case seems to me to have no probative value on the issues which arose.

4.19 Delay in forwarding a copy of the certificate A delay in furnishing the bureau's certificate until the commencement of the court case has proved fatal to the prosecution. Thus in *State (O'Regan) v. Plunkett*[73] the copy certificate when sent to the address furnished by the defendant was returned to the bureau by the postal service. The fact that it had been returned was notified to the gardaí, but for four months they took no steps to furnish it to the defendant. A summons was issued and served on the defendant, and when it came on for hearing the prosecuting garda sought an adjournment which was granted. The copy certificate was finally furnished to the defendant immediately before the commencement of the adjourned hearing. On an application to make absolute a conditional order of certiorari it was held that there had been a deliberate decision to withhold the certificate from the defendant and that the conditional order should be made absolute. Gannon J, in the course of his judgment, approved the following passage from the judgment of Finlay P (as he then was) in *State (Walshe) v. Murphy*:[74]

> I am satisfied that there is an obligation on the prosecuting authorities in a charge under section 49 of the Road Traffic Act 1961, where

---

71 Unreported judgment of the High Court (Finlay P, as he then was) delivered 27 November 1981.
72 At p. 6 of the judgment.
73 [1984] ILRM 347.
74 [1981] IR 275, 293-294 where a copy of the bureau's certificate had not been furnished to the defendant notwithstanding repeated requests.

they become specifically aware that the person charged has not received a copy of the certificate and requires one, to supply him with one in such good time as to provide him with a realistic opportunity to have the specimen which he has retained analysed and to contest the validity or correctness of the certificate which was issued. It does not seem to me that the possibility of an adjournment (which was not sought in this case and which the first respondent says he would have granted) cures a failure to comply with that basic requirement of natural justice where the hearing of the charge is almost two years later than the taking of the original specimen. I accept the contention made on behalf of the prosecutor that this Court has no way of knowing whether a specimen taken in August 1979, would be capable of any accurate or probative analysis in May 1981, and that therefore there is a fundamental want of fair procedure in the refusal or failure of the prosecuting authorities to supply a copy of the certificate upon demand and request — and I emphasise the necessity for that in order to invoke the concept of natural justice. On this ground alone, even if all other grounds urged on behalf of the prosecutor had failed, I would have been satisfied to disallow the cause shown.

4.20 It should not be inferred from the decisions in *State (O'Regan) v. Plunkett* and *State (Walshe) v. Murphy* that there is a general duty on the bureau to ensure that its certificate is actually received by the defendant. In *Director of Public Prosecutions v. McGuoy*[75] the certificate had been sent to the defendant by registered post but was returned to the gardaí with a note that it had been undelivered. The case was adjourned and the defendant's solicitors wrote to the bureau requesting a copy of the certificate. The certificate was then furnished to the defendant. It was held in the District Court that the bureau had failed to comply with its obligation to forward a copy of the certificate to the defendant as soon as practicable, and the charge against her was dismissed. On a case stated it was held in the High Court that the District Justice erred in law in dismissing the case. Finlay P (as he then was) held[76] that:

> the obligation imposed upon the Bureau is an obligation to forward a copy of the certificate of analysis. I must construe this as imposing upon them an obligation to take appropriate and practical steps to

---

75 Unreported judgment of the High Court (Finlay P, as he then was) delivered 25 July 1983.
76 At pp. 6-7 of the judgment.

send or cause to be delivered to a person whose sample of blood has been analysed a copy of the certificate . . . I cannot construe the obligation to forward a copy of the certificate as being equivalent to an absolute obligation to ensure its receipt by the party concerned.

The judge also held that, in considering whether the bureau had failed in its obligation to forward a copy of its certificate, a court is entitled to have regard to the consequences of any delay that occurred. And since the defendant had not, in this case, taken one of the samples in order to have it analysed, there could be no prejudice to her arising out of the delay in obtaining the certificate. The same conclusion was reached in *Director of Public Prosecutions v. Walsh*[77] where it was held that the mere fact that a defendant had not received delivery of a copy of the bureau's certificate did not affect its evidential value. In that case the copy certificate had been sent to the defendant by registered post but was returned to the bureau marked 'not collected'. No further effort was made to have the copy certificate delivered. On a case stated to the High Court, Gannon J held that the District Justice was wrong in law in dismissing the charge. He held that the defendant could not rely on the principles laid down in *State (Walshe) v. Murphy* and *State (O'Regan) v. Plunkett* where no evidence had been offered by or on his behalf. He pointed out[78] that: 'In both of those cases there was evidence given by or on behalf of the accused from which the court could infer that an injustice might be done despite the apparent compliance with formal procedures.'[79]

4.21 The critical factor seems to be whether the defendant has taken a sample. In *Hanratty v. Kirby*[80] the defendant's copy of the bureau's certificate, which had been sent to him by registered post, was returned to the bureau and the envelope marked 'not called for'. The prosecuting garda made a number of attempts, without success, to serve the copy certificate. When the case came on for hearing in the District Court the defendant's counsel sought an adjournment which was granted. The copy certificate was furnished to the defendant a few minutes before the adjourned hearing, and at the hearing his counsel sought a dismiss, citing *State (Walshe) v. Murphy* and *State (O'Regan) v. Plunkett*. The District

---

77 [1985] ILRM 243.
78 At p. 248 of the report.
79 The decisions in *Director of Public Prosecutions v. McGuoy* and *Director of Public Prosecutions v. Walsh* were applied in *Director of Public Prosecutions v. Connors* [1992] 2 IR 125.
80 Unreported judgment of the High Court (Keane J) delivered 22 July 1993.

Judge offered to adjourn the proceedings, but his offer was declined; he proceeded to hear the evidence and convicted the defendant. On the defendant's application for an order of certiorari by way of judicial review it was held that *State (Walshe) v. Murphy* and *State (O'Regan) v. Plunkett* were distinguishable because in those cases the defendant had retained a specimen: and since in the present case he had not retained a specimen, the delay in furnishing the certificate had no bearing on his obtaining an accurate analysis of the specimen, and so consideration of the requirements of natural justice did not arise. The application for judicial review was accordingly refused.

THE INOXIMETER

4.22 The requirement to provide two breath specimens As we have seen, a garda may, instead of or in addition to requiring the provision of a blood or urine specimen, require an arrested person to provide two specimens of his breath by exhaling into an apparatus for determining the concentration of alcohol in the breath.[81] Refusal or failure to comply forthwith with such a requirement is an offence, unless there is a special and substantial reason for the refusal or failure and the person complies (or offers, but is not called upon, to comply) with a requirement in relation to the taking of a blood specimen or the provision of a urine specimen.[82] The apparatus will determine the concentration of alcohol in each of the two specimens. If it determines that one of the specimens has a lower concentration than the other, then the specimen with the lower concentration is to be taken into account for the purposes of charges under sections 49 or 50.[83] If each specimen has the same concentration, then either specimen may be taken into account.[84]

4.23 The statements If the apparatus determines in respect of the specimen to be taken into account that the person may have contravened section 49(4) or 50(4) of the 1961 Act (the concentration of alcohol in his

---

81 Section 13(1) of the 1994 Act. In a prosecution for an offence under part III of the 1994 Act or under section 49 or 50 or the 1961 Act it is presumed, until the contrary is shown, that an apparatus provided by a member of the Garda Síochána for the purpose of enabling a person to provide two specimens of breath pursuant to the section is an apparatus for determining the concentration of alcohol in the breath: section 13(4) of the 1994 Act.

82 Section 13(2) and section 23(1) of the 1994 Act; and see para. 4.07 supra with regard to a special and substantial reason.

83 Section 17(1) of the 1994 Act.

84 Ibid.

breath exceeding 35 microgrammes of alcohol per 100 millilitres of breath), he is to be supplied forthwith by a member of the Garda Síochána with two identical statements, automatically produced by the apparatus in the prescribed form and duly completed by the member in the prescribed manner, stating the concentration of alcohol in the specimen.[85] On receipt of the statements the person is required, on being requested by the garda to do so, to acknowledge forthwith the receipt by placing his signature on each statement and return either of the statements to the garda.[86] Refusal or failure to comply with these requirements is an offence.[87]

4.24 The evidential value of a statement A duly completed statement purporting to have been supplied under section 17 is, until the contrary is shown, sufficient evidence in any proceedings under the Road Traffic Acts, 1961 to 1994 of the facts stated in it.[88] It is not necessary to prove any signature on it nor that the signatory was the proper person to sign it.[89] Furthermore, the statement is, until the contrary is shown, sufficient evidence of compliance by the member of the Garda Síochána concerned with the requirements imposed on him by or under part III of the 1994 Act prior to and and in connection with the supply by him of the statement.[90] The foregoing presumptions apply to a statement notwithstanding the fact that there has been a failure to comply with the requirements of section 17(3)(a), that is to say, notwithstanding a failure on the part of the defendant to acknowledge receipt of the statements by signing both of them.[91]

---

85 Section 17(2) of the 1994 Act.
86 Section 17(3) of the 1994 Act.
87 Section 17(4) of the 1994 Act.
88 Section 21(1) of the 1994 Act.

89 Ibid.
90 Ibid.
91 Section 17(5) of the 1994 Act.

5

The Doctor's Form, the Bureau's Certificate and the Designated Doctor

5.01 The doctor's form It has been held by the Supreme Court that production of the doctor's form is an essential proof in a prosecution under section 49(2) or (3) of the 1961 Act.[1] The 1994 Act provides that the duly completed form is, until the contrary is shown, sufficient evidence in any proceedings under the Road Traffic Acts, 1961 to 1994, of the facts stated in it.[2] It is not necessary to prove any signature on the form or that the signatory was the proper person to sign it.[3] The form is also, until the contrary is shown, sufficient evidence of compliance by the designated doctor concerned with the requirements imposed on him by or under part III of the 1994 Act.[4]

5.02 The bureau's certificate Production of the bureau's certificate is an essential proof in a prosecution under section 49(2) or (3) of the 1961 Act. The certificate is, until the contrary is shown, sufficient evidence in any proceedings under the Road Traffic Acts, 1961 to 1994, of the facts stated in it.[5] There is no need to prove any signature on it or that the signatory was the proper person to sign it.[6] The certificate is also, until the contrary is shown, sufficient evidence of compliance by the bureau with the requirements imposed on it by or under part III of the 1994 Act or part V of the 1968 Act.[7]

5.03 The evidential value of the certificate The certificate is evidence of the facts stated in it. But as can be seen from the prescribed form

---

[1] *Treacy v. Young*, unwritten decision of the Supreme Court, judgment delivered 13 July 1983.
[2] Section 21(2).
[3] Ibid.
[4] Ibid.
[5] Section 21(3) of the 1994 Act.
[6] Ibid.
[7] Ibid.

for the certificate,[8] it states a concentration of alcohol in the blood or urine 'on analysis'. The argument was advanced by the defendant in *Director of Public Prosecutions v. Smyth*[9] that since the certificate showed the concentration only at the time of analysis, there was no evidence before the court as to the concentration at the time of driving or within three hours of driving, and so there should be no conviction. Rejecting the argument, Blayney J held[10] that:

> The certificate in this case certifies that the concentration of alcohol in the specimen of the defendant's blood exceeded the statutory limit. That specimen had been taken from the defendant within the period of three hours after he had been observed driving by Garda Anthony Ferris. So the specimen taken, when analysed four days later, disclosed an excessive concentration of alcohol. In my opinion that is prima facie evidence that the concentration of alcohol in the defendant's blood within the relevant three hours exceeded the statutory limit. What was analysed was the specimen taken. If the defendant alleged that the specimen had altered between the time it was taken and the time it was analysed, that case could be made by way of rebuttal of the prosecutor's prima facie case, but in my opinion there was no onus on the prosecution to prove that no change had taken place. What is in issue is whether the prosecution has established a prima facie case, in other words, whether it has proved facts on the strength of which, if this were a jury trial, a jury would be entitled to convict. In my opinion the prosecution has established this.

5.04 In the *Director of Public Prosecutions v. Collins*[11] the evidence disclosed that the two containers into which the doctor had put the blood specimen contained an unspecified white substance. The Supreme Court rejected the contention that there was an onus on the prosecution to disprove the possibility that the white substance had been put into the containers in error and had distorted the result of the analysis. The court relied on the evidential value of the bureau's certificate under section 23(2) of the 1978 Act which corresponds to section 21(3) of the 1994 Act. It was held that the onus of showing that the analysis was capable of being

---

8 Set out in the Road Traffic Act 1994 (Part III) Regulations, 1994, SI No. 351 of 1994; see appendix C.

9 [1987] ILRM 570.
10 At p. 574 of the report.
11 [1981] ILRM 447.

rendered false by the unspecified white substance lay on the defendant; and since the defendant had failed to adduce any evidence to show that the substance found in the containers could have falsified the analysis, he had failed to discharge that onus. It was pointed out that, even if such evidence had been adduced, the prosecution would have been entitled to give rebutting evidence.

5.05 The signature on the certificate The prescribed form for the bureau's certificate requires the signature of the 'person who carried out the analysis' to be placed on the certificate. In *Hobbs v. Hurley*[12] evidence given on behalf of the defendant by the analyst whose signature appeared on the bureau's certificate disclosed that the analysis of the specimen involved the carrying out of two tests, the calculation of a mean of the results of those two tests, and the deduction of 6 per cent. from that mean to give the figure shown in the certificate. In that case the first test had been deducted by the analyst herself and the second test had been done by a colleague of hers. The validity of the certificate was challenged on the grounds that it had been signed by only one of the two persons whose separate actions comprised the bureau's analysis of the specimen and that the figure certified was based on hearsay as the calculation which produced it was made by someone who had not carried out the two tests, and who was therefore dependent on information obtained from someone else. Costello J (as he then was) rejected both arguments. In relation to the hearsay argument, he held[13] that since 'the Bureau is a body corporate and acts through its authorised officers and agents it cannot be said that the certificate is based on hearsay evidence — it is based on knowledge acquired by the Bureau in the same way as any body corporate acquires knowledge.' And in relation to the other argument, he pointed out[14] that:

> Section 22 (of the 1978 Act, now section 19 of the 1994 Act) makes a distinction between an analysis of the specimen the Bureau receives and the determination of the concentration of alcohol in it and it seems me to that the second test which took place in this case can properly be regarded as part of the process . . . to enable the determination to be made by the Bureau, and that the person who carried out the first test can be properly regarded as the person who

---

12 Unreported judgment of the High Court (Costello J, as he then was) delivered 10 June 1980.

13 At p. 20 of the judgment.

14 At pp. 20-21 of the judgment.

carried out the analysis. Secondly, it appears from the facts set out in the Case that the procedures of the Bureau envisage that one analyst in the Bureau is to have charge of each case, and this is the person who not only carries out a test on the specimen but also checks the documents after they have been typed up and returned from the typing office. The analyst with this particular responsibility can, it seems to me, validly sign the certificate as a person who carried out the analysis.

5.06 The legibility of the signature on the bureau's certificate was considered in *Director of Public Prosections v. Collins*.[15] The Circuit Court judge found that the signature of the person who purported to sign the bureau's certificate as director or deputy director or other duly authorised officer was illegible. On a case stated the Supreme Court held that this finding was not binding on it. Henchy J held[16] that even if he 'agreed with the judge's finding of illegibility, that finding would not detract from the validity of what is clearly intended to be a handwritten signature. Legibility is not a hallmark of an effective signature.' Henchy J went on to point out that the 'form does not require (a signatory) to specify the precise one of the permitted capacities in which he may sign'. He held that:[17]

> Because of the terms of section 23(2) (now section 21(3) of the 1994 Act), the onus lay on the defendant to show that one or other, or both, of (the) signatories did not sign in one or other of the capacities which the printed form allowed each to sign. Since no such evidence was adduced by the defendant, section 23(2) deprives him of the standing to complain that the certificate lacks full validity.

5.07 **Errors in the form or certificate** The effect of relatively minor errors in the completion of the doctor's form has already been considered.[18] But there have been cases involving more substantive errors. In *Director of Public Prosecutions v. McPartland*[19] where the bureau's certificate incorrectly stated the defendant's address, it was held that the District Judge erred in law in finding that there was no evidence that the defendant

---

15 [1981] ILRM 447. The decision in *Collins* on this point was applied in *Director of Public Prosecutons v O'Neill*, unreported decision of the Supreme Court, judgment of Hederman J delivered 30 July 1984.

16 At p. 455 of the report.
17 Ibid.
18 Paras. 4.10-4.11 ante and see *Director of Public Prosecutions v. Flahive* [1988] ILRM 133.
19 [1983] ILRM 411.

was the person named in the certificate. In reaching this conclusion the court relied on the fact that the summons served on the defendant bore substantially the same and equally incorrect address, and that the defendant duly appeared in court in response to the summons.[20] Even more fundamental are errors in the defendant's name. In *Director of Public Prosecutions v. Cullen*,[21] for example, the bureau's certificate and the doctor's form referred to the defendant as 'John Curran' rather than 'John Cullen'. On a case stated to the High Court it was held that the District Judge erred in law in dismissing the charge. There was, however, evidence before the District Court that the discrepancy had resulted from an error by the doctor and that both documents, notwithstanding the error in them, referred to the the defendant; indeed, the District Judge would appear to have found as a fact that Cullen and Curran were one and the same person. Where an error occurs in the defendant's name, it is submitted that there should be no conviction unless there is evidence showing that the defendant and the person named are one and the same. If there is no such evidence, there should be no conviction.[22]

5.08 The defendant's entitlement to a copy of the doctor's form Unlike the case in relation to the certificate, the 1994 Act makes no provision for furnishing of a copy of the doctor's form to the defendant. In *State (Higgins) v. Reid*[23] the defendant's solicitor sought a copy of the form in advance of the hearing. On an application to make absolute a conditional order of mandamus it was held that the issue was one for the consideration of the court before which the prosecution was pending. This conclusion probably still represents the law.[24]

5.09 The regulations The Minister for the Environment is empowered to make regulations for the purpose of giving effect to the 1994 Act.[25] Under this power the Road Traffic Act 1994 (Part III) Regulations, 1994[26] have been made providing for the form to be completed by the designated

---

20 That the court should rely on such matters in order to conclude that the defendant and the person referred to in the certificate were one and the same person seems questionable; *McPartland* may be of doubtful authority.
21 Unwritten judgment of the High Court (Barron J) delivered 2 July 1984.
22 *Director of Public Prosecutions v. Tuttle* unwritten judgment of the High Court (Barrington J) delivered 23 March 1987, *Irish Times*, 24 March 1987.
23 [1983] ILRM 310.
24 See *Director of Public Prosecutions v. Doyle* [1994] 2 IR 286; [1994] 1 ILRM 529.
25 Section 3(1) of the 1994 Act.
26 SI No. 351 of 1994.

doctor and the certificate to be issued by the bureau.[27] In *Director of Public Prosecutions v. Collins*[28] it was held that a judge was entitled to take judicial notice of the corresponding regulations made under the 1978 Act, and so it was not necessary to produce them in court.

5.10 The designated doctor In a prosecution for an offence under section 49 or 50 of the 1961 Act or section 13, 14 or 15 of the 1994 Act it is presumed, until the contrary is shown, that each of the following is a designated doctor.[29]

1. A person who by virtue of powers conferred on him by part III of the 1994 Act took from another person a specimen of his blood or was provided by another person with a specimen of his urine.

2. A person for whom, following a requirement under section 13(1), 14(4), or 15(1) to permit the taking by him of a specimen of blood, there was a refusal or failure to give such permission or to comply with a requirement of his in relation to the taking of such a specimen.

3. A person for whom, following a requirement under section 13(1), 14(4) or 15(1) to provide for him a specimen of urine, there was a refusal or failure to provide such a specimen or to comply with a requirement of his in relation to the provision of such a specimen.

5.11 The existence of this presumption obviates the need to prove that the person summoned by the gardaí to take a specimen is a designated doctor.[30] In *O'Connor v Bannon*[31] it was held that the presumption lawfully arose where the doctor had taken the specimen following a requirement by a garda under section 13(1)(b) (of the 1978 Act) and the designation by the garda of the doctor to take the specimen. The presumption that certain persons are designated doctors now applies in the case of a charge of refusal or failure to give a specimen under section 13, and not just to a prosecution for drunken driving under section 49 or for being drunk in charge under section 50 as was the case under the 1978 Act. Consequently, it is no longer

---

27 See appendix C.
28 [1981] ILRM 447.
29 Section 21(4) of the 1994 Act. 'Doctor' means a person registered in the General Register of Medical Practitioners established under section 26 of the Medical Practitioners Act 1978: section 9(1) of the 1994 Act.
30 'Designated' for this purpose means designated by a member of the Garda Síochána: section 9(1) of the 1994 Act.
31 Unreported judgment of the High Court (McMahon J) delivered 15 December 1980.

necessary, in a prosecution for refusal or failure to give a specimen, for evidence to be given that the doctor was at the material time on the register of medical practitioners.[32]

---

32 A requirement which gave rise to difficulties in the past: see *Director of Public Prosecutions v. Haughey*, unreported judgment of the District Court (District Judge Hamill) delivered 7 September 1990; *Director of Public Prosecutions v. O'Donoghue* [1991] 1 IR 448.

6

Penalties

FINES AND IMPRISONMENT

6.01 Fines Normally conviction for a drunken driving offence will result in the imposition of a fine. When fixing the amount of the fine the judge is required to take into consideration the means of the offender.[1] He may fix the period for payment; if no period is fixed, the fine must be paid on the expiration of seven clear days from date of the order.[2] The judge may order that the fine be paid forthwith if satisfied that the offender is possessed of sufficient means to enable him to pay forthwith; or that the offender has no fixed abode within his jurisdiction; or if the offender on being asked if he desires time for payment, does not express any such desire; or if there is any other special reason.[3] Section 2 of the Courts (No. 2) Act 1986 provides that where on summary conviction a fine is imposed a court may order that, in default of due payment of the fine, the person liable should be imprisoned for a term not exceeding the appropriate period specified in the following scale:

Amount of fine	*Period of imprisonment*
Not exceeding £50	5 days
Exceeding £50 but not exceeding £250	15 days
Exceeding £250 but not exceeding £500	45 days
Exceeding £500	90 days

6.02 In *State (Delaney) v. Magee*[4] it was argued that a District Court order was made in excess of jurisdiction where the defendant was convicted under section 49 of the 1961 Act and sentenced to three months imprisonment and fined £250 with three months to pay and, in default of payment, was ordered to be imprisoned for a period of six months. Because the maximum permissible sentence was six months, the defendant con-

---

[1] DCR, 1948 r. 65(1)(a).
[2] DCR, 1948 r. 65(1)(b).
[3] Ibid.
[4] [1983] ILRM 45.

tended that the order was bad in that it effectively made him liable to imprisonment for nine months. The High Court held that imprisonment for non-payment of the fine was of a different character from imprisonment as punishment for the offence; consequently, the defendant was not exposed to any greater punishment than that prescribed by the statute.

6.03 Where a fine has been imposed and time is allowed for payment, the clerk must send a notice to the defendant stating that the fine has been imposed, its amount and the time within which it is to be paid and notifying him that if he fails to pay a warrant will issue.[5] The notice may be sent by ordinary post to the defendant at his last known or usual place of abode.[6] The failure to comply with this requirement will not prejudice the issue of a warrant.[7]

6.04 **Imprisonment** A defendant may be sentenced to a term of imprisonment for a drunken driving offence.[8] But there should be no automatic sentence of imprisonment and each case should be determined on its own merits.[9] In *Attorney General v. Greene*[10] the defendant, the driver of a CIE bus, appealed to the Circuit Court in respect of a sentence of three months' imprisonment imposed for drunken driving under section 30 of the Road Traffic Act 1933. Affirming the sentence, Judge McCarthy said:[11]

> I have stated frequently in this Court that in my view drunken drivers should be sent to prison unless there are mitigating and extenuating circumstances and my colleagues and I have, whenever they really exist, given defendants the benefit thereof. I believe that in the spirit of the Statute the legislature did not enact that all drunken drivers be sent to prison. It gave the adjudicating tribunal a wide discretion. ... My interpretation of that section is that mitigating or extenuating circumstances must get full consideration. There may be age, sex, health, the degrees of incapacity, the deliberation by which incapacity was produced, the general conduct, the time, the place, the opportunity, inducements, other attendant circumstances and the length of time driving. As well, of course, one must consider the frequency of

---

5 DCR, 1948 r. 65(7) as added by District Court Rules (No. 1), 1962 SI No. 7 of 1962.
6 Ibid.
7 Ibid.
8 See paras. 6.09-6.13 infra for the penalties provided under the 1994 Act.
9 *Heffron v. Hughes* [1949] Ir Jur Rep 58.
10 (1952) 86 ILTR 31.
11 At p. 32 of the report.

the offence and the question of what harm may be done. These are only some of the circumstances which a tribunal has to consider and which must be judicially examined.

DISQUALIFICATIONS

6.05 Types of disqualification The 1961 Road Traffic Act, as amended, provides for three different types of order disqualifying a person from holding a driving licence: consequential, ancillary and special disqualification orders. A consequential disqualification order is a mandatory order which generally must be made whenever a person is convicted of an offence set out in the second schedule to the 1961 Act.[12] An ancillary disqualification order, on the other hand, is a discretionary order which may be made where a person is convicted of an offence under the Road Traffic Act or otherwise in relation to a mechanically propelled vehicle or the driving of such a vehicle (other than an offence carrying a consequential disqualification) or of a crime or offence in the commission of which a mechanically propelled vehicle has been used.[13] A judge imposing such a disqualification may disqualify for a specified period or for a specified period and thereafter until the offender has produced to the appropriate licensing authority a certificate of competency or a certificate of fitness or both.[14] The imposition of an ancillary disqualification order, it has been held, entails a finding that the offender is unfit to hold a driving licence and the question of disqualification should be judicially determined upon the appropriate evidence; such a disqualification should not be treated as the imposition of an additional punishment.[15] Finally, a special disqualifi-

---

12 Section 26(1) of the 1961 Act as substituted by section 26 of the 1994 Act.
13 Section 27(1)(a) of the 1961 Act.
14 Section 27(1)(b) of the 1961 Act.
15 'One must not lose sight . . . of the real nature of the disqualification order which is that it is essentially a finding of unfitness of the person concerned to hold a driving licence. Apart from the statutory minimum which is imposed in certain cases, this is a matter which must be determined by the Court in the light of evidence which it hears on this aspect of the case and in the light of that evidence it may determine what period of disqualification will be appropriate. A motor car, if not driven properly, is a potential danger not merely to the driver himself but to all other persons using the highway. It is obvious that the protection of the common good requires that the right to drive a motor car cannot be unrestricted. The right may therefore be lost if a Court, on a consideration of the relevant facts and materials, determines that the person concerned, by reason of his general recklessness or thoughtlessness or of his propensity to drink, or by reason of disease or other disability or his abuse of the right by exercising it in the further-

cation order may be made on application to a judge of the District Court where an officer of the Garda Síochána has reasonable grounds to believe that the holder of a driving licence is by reason of disease or physical or mental disability unfit to drive or is incompetent to drive.[16] Such a disqualification order disqualifies the person from holding a driving licence until he produces to the appropriate licensing authority a certificate of fitness in a case of disqualification for disease or disability or a certificate of competency in a case of disqualification for incompetence.[17]

6.06 Operation of the disqualification A person in respect of whom a disqualification order has been made is disqualified in accordance with the order from holding a driving licence and a driving licence held by him stands suspended correspondingly.[18] A special disqualification order comes into operation immediately it is made and a consequential or ancillary order comes into operation on the fifteenth day after it is made.[19] The operation of a consequential or ancillary order may be postponed for a period not exceeding six months, but only if the court is satisfied that a special reason relating to the circumstances of the convicted person has been proved by him to exist.[20]

6.07 Where a consequential or ancillary disqualification order, or the conviction to which it is related, is the subject of an appeal, notice of which has been lodged within 14 days and the convicted person has entered into a recognisance to prosecute the appeal, the operation of the order stands suspended pending the appeal.[21] But if the appeal is not prosecuted or the

---

ance of criminal activities, is unfit to exercise the right to drive a motor car. Such disqualification is not a punishment notwithstanding that the consequence of such finding of unfitness might be both socially and economically serious for the person concerned.' Per Walsh J in *Conroy v. Attorney General* [1965] IR 411, 441-442; see also *People (Attorney General) v. Poyning* [1972] IR 402 and *Joyce v. Circuit Court Judge for the Western Circuit* [1987] ILRM 316.

16 Section 28(1) and (2) of the 1961 Act. Section 28(1) has been amended by section 49(1)(c) of the 1994 Act so as to enable the appropriate licensing authority to make the application in a case of unfitness by reason of disease or physical or mental disability.
17 Ibid.
18 Section 30(1) of the 1961 Act as substituted by section 20 of the 1968 Act.
19 Section 30(3)(a) of the 1961 Act as substituted by section 20 of the 1968 Act.
20 Section 30(3)(d) and (e) of the 1961 Act as substituted by section 20 of the 1968 Act.
21 Section 30(3)(c) of the 1961 Act as substituted by 20 of the 1968 Act.

order is confirmed or varied by the appellate court, the period of disqualification begins on the day on which the appropriate order of the appellate court is made, unless a postponement is granted.[22] Should the appellant give notification in writing that he wishes to withdraw his appeal, the suspension of the operation of the order terminates immediately before the day on which notification was given and the period of disqualification begins on that day.[23]

6.08 Removal of the disqualification A person in respect of whom a consequential disqualification order has been made may apply, after three months from the beginning of the period of disqualification, to the court which made the order for the removal of the disqualification.[24] The court may remove the disqualification as and from a specified date not earlier than six months after the beginning of the period of disqualification if it considers that circumstances exist which justify such a course.[25] But if the consequential disqualification order was made on conviction for an offence to which section 26(4) or (5) of the 1961 Act, as inserted by section 26 of the 1994 Act, applies (ie, among other offences, drunken driving, drunk in charge, or refusals or failures to provide specimens under sections 13, 14 or 15 of the 1994 Act), and the period of disqualification was not less than two years, the person may not apply until after the expiration of nine months from the beginning of the period of disqualification and the court may not remove the disqualification as from a date earlier than one year after the beginning of the period of disqualification; and if it does remove the disqualification, the court must order the person to comply with any requirement contained in the disqualification order for the production of a certificate or certificates to the appropriate licensing authority.[26] In the case of a four year period of disqualification, the person may not apply until after the expiration of 21 months from the beginning of the period

---

22 Section 30(5) of the 1961 Act as substituted by section 20 of the 1968 Act.
23 Section 30(4) of the 1961 Act as substituted by section 20 of the 1968 Act.
24 Section 29(1)(a) of the 1961 Act as substituted by section 19 of the 1968 Act. In the case of an order varied on appeal, the application must be made to the appellate court: section 29(3) of the 1961 Act.
25 Section 29(1)(a) of the 1961 Act as substituted by section 19 of the 1968 Act. In the case of an ancillary disqualification order specifying a period of disqualification exceeding three months, application may be made after the expiration of two months from the beginning of the period of disqualification for the removal of the disqualification on a specified date not earlier than three months after the beginning of the period: section 29(1)(b) of the 1961 Act as substituted by section 19 of the 1968 Act.
26 Section 29(1A)(a) of the 1961 Act as inserted by section 27 of the 1994 Act.

Penalties 77

of disqualification and the court may not remove the disqualification as from a date earlier than two years after the beginning of the disqualification.[27] In considering whether circumstances exist justifying the removal of a disqualification order the court may have regard to all matters which appear to it to be relevant and may, in particular, have regard to the character of the applicant, his conduct after conviction and the nature of his offence.[28] If the application is refused, a fresh application may not be made for three months.[29] An appeal lies against a refusal or if the applicant is aggrieved by the date as from which the disqualification is removed.[30]

The remainder of this chapter sets out the penalties for the various offences considered elsewhere in this book.

SECTIONS 49 AND 50 OF THE 1961 ACT: DRUNKEN DRIVING AND DRUNK IN CHARGE

6.09 A person convicted of an offence under sections 49 or 50 of the 1961 Act is liable to a fine not exceeding £1,000 and/or imprisonment for a term not exceeding six months.[31] Section 1(1) of the Probation of Offenders Act 1907 does not apply to offences under the sections.[32] On conviction the court must make a consequential disqualification order declaring the person disqualified from holding a driving licence.[33] The court must order that particulars of the conviction and disqualification be endorsed on the defendant's driving licence.[34] The minimum period of disqualification, on conviction for an offence under section 49(1) or 50(1), is two years in the case of a first offence and four years in the case of a second or subsequent offence.[35] On conviction for an offence under section 49(2), (3) or (4) or section 50(2), (3) or (4) the minimum period of disqualification in the case of a first offence is to be not less than the appropriate period specified in column (3) of the table set out below and in the case of a second or subsequent offence not less than the period set out in column (4) of the

---

27 Section 29(1A)(b) of the 1961 Act as inserted by section 27 of the 1994 Act.
28 Section 29(2) of the 1961 Act.
29 Section 29(5) of the 1961 Act.
30 Section 29(6) of the 1961 Act.
31 Section 49(6)(a) of the 1961 Act as inserted by section 10 of the 1994 Act and section 50(6)(a) of the 1961 Act as inserted by section 11 of the 1994 Act.
32 Section 49(7) of the 1961 Act as inserted by section 10 of the 1994 Act and section 50(7) of the 1961 Act as inserted by section 11 of the 1994 Act.
33 Section 26(1) of the 1961 Act as substituted by section 26 of the 1994 Act and the second schedule to the 1961 Act as substituted by section 49(1)(l) of the 1994 Act.
34 Section 36(3)(a) of the 1961 Act.
35 Section 26(4)(a) of the 1961 Act as substituted by section 2 of the 1995 Act.

TABLE

Reference Number (1)	Concentration of alcohol (2)	First offence under the section concerned (3)	Second or any subsequent offence under the same section (4)
1.	(a) Not exceeding 100 milligrammes of alcohol per 100 millilitres of blood; (b) Not exceeding 135 milligrammes of alcohol per 100 millilitres of urine; (c) Not exceeding 44 microgrammes of alcohol per 100 millilitres of breath.	3 months	6 months
2.	(a) Exceeding 100 milligrammes but not exceeding 150 milligrammes of alcohol per 100 millilitres of blood; (b) Exceeding 135 milligrammes but not exceeding 200 milligrammes of alcohol per 100 millilitres of urine; (c) Exceeding 44 milligrammes but not exceeding 66 microgrammes of alcohol per 100 millilitres of breath.	1 year	2 years
3.	(a) Exceeding 150 milligrammes of alcohol per 100 millilitres of blood; (b) Exceeding 200 milligrammes of alcohol per 100 millilitres of urine. (c) Exceeding 66 microgrammes of alcohol per 100 millilitres of breath.	2 years	4 years

table.[36] Where a person who has previously been convicted of an offence under sections 49 or 50 of the 1961 Act, or under sections 13, 14 or 17 of the 1978 Act, or under sections 13, 14 or 15 of the 1994 Act, is convicted of an offence under sections 49 or 50, the later conviction will be regarded

36 Section 26(4)(b) of the 1961 Act as substituted by section 2 of the 1995 Act.

Penalties 79

as a second or, as the case may be, a subsequent conviction for the purpose of disqualification.[37] But where a period of four years or more during which the person was not disqualified from holding a licence has elapsed since the last previous conviction, the court may deal with the later of the two convictions as a first conviction.[38] A person convicted of an offence under sections 49 or 50 committed after the commencement of the drunken driving provisions of the 1994 Act on 2 December 1994, but before the passing of the 1995 Act on 25 May 1995, may apply to the court which disqualified him for an order substituting the appropriate period of disqualification under the 1995 Act for the period imposed on him and removing the requirement that he remain disqualified until he produces a certificate of competency.[39]

SECTION 12 OF THE 1994 ACT: REFUSAL OR FAILURE TO COMPLY WITH A BREATHALYSER

6.10 Conviction under section 12 of the 1994 Act renders the defendant liable to a fine not exceeding £1,000 and/or imprisonment for a term not exceeding six months.[40] There is no provision for a consequential disqualification order for an offence under the section.

SECTIONS 13, 14 AND 15 OF THE 1994 ACT: REFUSAL OR FAILURE TO COMPLY WITH A REQUIREMENT IN RELATION TO A SPECIMEN

6.11 A person convicted of an offence under sections 13, 14 or 15 of the 1994 Act is liable to a fine not exceeding £1,000 and/or imprisonment for a term not exceeding six months.[41] Section 1(1) of the Probation of Offenders Act 1907 does not apply to offences under the sections.[42] On conviction the court must make a consequential disqualification order declaring the person disqualified from holding a driving licence.[43] The court must order that particulars of the conviction and disqualification be endorsed on the defendant's driving licence.[44] The minimum period of

---

37 Section 26(6) of the 1961 Act as substituted by section 26 of the 1994 Act.
38 Section 26(8) of the 1961 Act as substituted by section 26 of the 1994 Act.
39 Section 3 of the Road Traffic Act 1995.
40 Section 12(2) of the 1994 Act.
41 Sections 13(2) and (3), 14(2) and (5) and 15(2) of the 1994 Act.

42 Sections 13(5), 14(6) and 15(4) of the 1994 Act.
43 Section 26(1) of the 1961 Act as substituted by section 26 of the 1994 Act and the second schedule to the 1961 Act as substituted by section 49(1)(l) of the 1994 Act.
44 Section 36(3)(a) of the 1961 Act.

disqualification is two years in the case of a first offence and four years in the case of a second or subsequent offence.[45] Where a person who has previously been convicted of an offence under sections 49 or 50 of the 1961 Act, or under sections 13, 14 or 17 of the 1978 Act, or under sections 13, 14 or 15 of the 1994 Act, is convicted of an offence under sections 13, 14 or 15, the later conviction will be regarded as a second or, as the case may be, a subsequent conviction for the purpose of disqualification.[46] But where a period of four years or more during which the person was not disqualified from holding a licence has elapsed since the last previous conviction, the court may deal with the later of the two convictions as a first conviction.[47]

SECTION 17 OF THE 1994 ACT: REFUSAL OR FAILURE TO ACKNOWLEDGE AND RETURN A STATEMENT

6.12 On conviction for an offence under section 17(4) the defendant is liable to a fine not exceeding £500 and/or imprisonment for a term not exceeding three months.[48] There is no provision for a consequential disqualification order for an offence under the section.

SECTION 20 OF THE 1994 ACT: FRUSTRATING A PROSECUTION

6.13 On conviction for an offence under section 20(3)(a) the defendant is liable to a fine not exceeding £1,000 and/or imprisonment for a term not exceeding six months.[49] There is no provision for a consequential disqualification order for an offence under the section.

---

45 Section 26(4)(a) of the 1961 Act as substituted by section 2 of the 1995 Act.
46 Section 26(6) of the 1961 Act as substituted by section 26 of the 1994 Act.
47 Section 26(8) of the 1961 Act as substituted by section 26 of the 1994 Act.
48 Section 17(4) of the 1994 Act.
49 Section 20(3)(b) of the 1994 Act.

7

The Commencement of Charges

THE RIGHT TO PROSECUTE

7.01 The Director of Public Prosecutions has a general right to prosecute in cases of summary jurisdiction.[1] In addition, a member of the Garda Síochána may prosecute a case of drunken driving as a 'common informer', a term which, according to Kennedy CJ in *State (Cronin) v. The Circuit Court Judge of the Western Circuit*,[2] 'really means no more than a member of the public capable of giving information in respect of the commission of an offence'.[3] It was held there that a garda sergeant was competent to prosecute the defendant for being drunk in charge of a motor car. Once a garda initiates a charge as a common informer, it has been decided that neither the DPP nor the Attorney General is entitled to intervene to prevent the prosecution proceeding.[4] But the practice of gardaí prosecuting as common informers has been criticised in *People v. Roddy*[5] where Griffin J in the course of his judgment said:

> During the course of the argument, Mr Barrington drew attention to the undesirability of prosecutions which are essentially public prosecutions, paid for out of public funds, being brought in the name of

---

1 See the Criminal Justice (Administration) Act 1924, section 9(2) and the Prosecution of Offences Act 1974, section 3(1). See also *Attorney General v. Healy* [1928] IR 460. Where proceedings are initiated in his name alleging a summary offence, it was held in *People v. Roddy* [1977] IR 177 that the complainant should be the 'the Director of Public Prosecutions' simpliciter and not 'the People at the suit of the Director of Public Prosecutions'. It was also held that such proceedings did not require the prior authorisation of the Director of Public Prosecutions.

2 [1937] IR 34, 49.

3 The common informer does not, however, have to be an eyewitness to the events which give rise to the prosecution: *McCormack v. Carroll* (1911) 45 ILTR 7.

4 *State (Collins) v. Ruane* [1984] IR 105; [1985] ILRM 349.

5 [1977] IR 177, 190. See also Dwyer, 'The Garda as Prosecuting Advocate in the District Court', (1991) 9 ILT (NS) 89.

what has come to be known as the 'the prosecuting garda' as a common informer. In such cases, if a member of the Garda Síochána is to bring proceedings in his own name, he can do so only as a common informer. If the practice of bringing proceedings in the name of a member of the Garda Síochána is to be continued, it would be far more desirable that he should be given a statutory power to do so, rather than having to prosecute as a common informer. However, it would be more desirable still if all prosecutions were brought in the name of the Director of Public Prosecutions, if whatever administrative difficulties which now exist could be overcome.

It seems those difficulties have been overcome, as drunken driving prosecutions are now invariably prosecuted in the name of the Director of Public Prosecutions.

PROCEDURE BY SUMMONS

7.02 The two types of summons and their purpose Prosecutions for drunken driving are usually instituted by the issue of a summons. There are two different types of summons in use: those issued under the District Court Rules, 1948 and the Petty Sessions (Ireland) Act 1851 and those issued under the Courts (No. 3) Act 1986. The purpose of a summons was considered by Henchy J in *Director of Public Prosecutions v. Clein*[6] where he held that:

> A summons ... is only a written command issued to a defendant for the purpose of getting him to attend court on a specified date to answer a specified complaint. If he responds to that command by appearing in court on the specified date and by answering the summons when it is called in court, he cannot be heard to say that he was not properly summoned if the complaint set out in the summons is a valid one.

In *Clein's* case the summonses were issued bearing a particular date and were made returnable for another date. Both dates were changed to later dates, and the alterations were initialled by the peace commissioner who had issued the summonses. The defendant was represented when the summonses came on for hearing. It was held that, even if there had been

---

6 [1983] ILRM 76, 77. See also *Power v. Kirby*, unreported judgment of the High Court (Barron J) delivered 23 April 1986.

a breach of a procedural requirement, that breach was cured when the defendant appeared in court on the day specified for hearing. On the other hand, in *McGirl v. McArdle*,[7] the defendant did not appear in court in answer to a summons which was not in the form prescribed by the rules of court but was represented by a solicitor who indicated to the court that the defendant was not submitting to its jurisdiction. The District Judge issued a warrant for the defendant's arrest which on an application for judicial review was quashed; it was held that the appearance of the solicitor was not sufficient to cure the defective summons.

7.03 While breach of a procedural requirement may be cured by the appearance of the defendant, the same may not apply to breach of his constitutional rights. In *Coughlan v. Patwell*[8] the defendant, who appeared in the District Court in answer to summonses alleging offences under the Road Traffic Acts, complained that his name and address had been obtained in breach of his constitutional rights. The District Judge refused to hear his submission, told him that any application in relation to his constitutional rights should be made to the High Court and proceeded to convict. On the defendant's application for certiorari by way of judicial review it was held that the District Judge exceeded his jurisdiction in determining the case without having considered the defendant's submission; the convictions were quashed, but the case was remitted to the District Court with a direction that the defendant's submission should be heard. Denham J explained[9] that:

> Procedural errors in issuing summonses are cured by the appearance in court of the accused. However, at issue here is not a rule of procedure but an allegation of a breach of constitutional rights, and the right to make that allegation. . . . The District Court has a duty to act constitutionally and to act in such a manner as to preserve an individual's constitutional rights. If an individual as here alleges that his constitutional rights have been infringed in procedures adopted in bringing him before the court then the District Justice has jurisdiction to, and indeed should, hear the submission and take such steps as it considers proper.

7.04 Summonses issued under the District Court Rules 1948 and the Petty Sessions (Ireland) Act 1851 Rule 29 of the District Court

---

7 [1989] IR 596; [1989] ILRM 495.
8 [1993] 1 IR 31.
9 At pp. 35 and 37 of the report.

Rules provided that: 'When it is intended that a summons . . . only shall be issued in the first instance to require the attendance before the court of a person against whom a complaint is made, the complaint may be made to a Justice, a Peace Commissioner or a (District Court) Clerk, and may be made either with or without oath, and in writing or not, as the Justice, Peace Commissioner or Clerk shall direct.' Rule 30 empowered the District Justice, Peace Commissioner or District Court Clerk to issue a summons which 'shall direct the appearance of the defendant before a Justice who has jurisdiction to hear and determine the complaint'. The statutory basis for these provisions is to be found in sections 10 and 11 of the Petty Sessions (Ireland) Act 1851. Section 10 provided that: 'Whenever Information shall be given to any Justice that any Person has committed or is suspected to have committed any Treason, Felony, Misdemeanour, or other Offence, within the Limits of the Jurisdiction of such Justice, for which such Person shall be punishable either by Indictment or upon a Summary Conviction . . . or whenever a Complaint shall be made to any Justice as to any other matter arising within the Limits of his Jurisdiction, upon which he shall have Power to make a Summary Order, it shall be lawful for such Justice to receive such Information or Complaint, and to proceed in respect to the same. . . .' By section 11 it was provided that: 'In all cases of summary Jurisdiction the Justice may issue his Summons directed to such a Person, requiring him to appear and answer to the Complaint. . . .' In addition, section 11 required that a summons issued by a justice should be signed by him.

7.05 The Petty Sessions (Ireland) Act makes no mention of peace commissioners or District Court clerks. The post of peace commissioner was established by the Courts of Justice Act 1924 which provided that a peace commissioner should have the authority formerly vested in a justice of the peace to sign summonses. The office of District Court clerk was created by the Court Officers Act 1926. A clerk was, under section 48 of the Act, to 'have and exercise all such powers and authorities and perform and fulfil all such duties and functions in relation to the District Court in such district court area or areas as shall from time to time be conferred or imposed on him by statute or rule of court. . . . ' Analysis of these statutory provisions led Finlay CJ to observe in *State (Clarke) v. Roche*[10] that 'whereas the Peace Commissioner was given express statutory power to issue a summons, the District Court Clerk was not and that his authority

---

10 [1986] IR 619, 639; [1987] ILRM 309.

derives from the Rules of Court rather than from any statute, though there is a provision in the Act of 1926, giving him such authority as may be conferred on him by any rule of court'.

7.06 A direct challenge to the authority of a District Court clerk to issue a summons was made in *Rainey v. Delap*.[11] It was contended that the provisions of rules 29 and 30 of the District Court Rules, providing for the making of a complaint to a District Court clerk and the issue of a summons by him, were ultra vires the rule-making authority and unconstitutional in that they conferred on a clerk a judicial function in a criminal matter. The Supreme Court upheld the first contention. 'The effect of rr. 29 and 30 of the District Court Rules, 1948,' said Finlay CJ,[12] 'was to alter what had been the exclusive function of the justice of the peace under the Act of 1851 so as to provide an alternative officer for the carrying out of that function.... [T]he power conferred on the District Court rule-making authority to alter statutory provisions provided for in s. 91 of the Courts of Justice Act 1924, is confined to changes which are adaptations or modifications of a statute.... I am driven to the conclusion that to confer on a District Court clerk an identical power of receiving a complaint and deciding whether or not to issue a summons in a criminal case which by virtue of a statute was heretofore confined to a justice of the peace and subsequently by transference to a district justice, goes far beyond an adaptation or modification of the Act of 1851 necessary for any of the purposes connected with practice and procedure which are mentioned in section 91 of the Courts of Justice Act 1924.' Having decided that rules 29 and 30 were invalid insofar as they granted to a District Court clerk powers to receive a complaint and issue a summons, the Supreme Court decided it was not then necessary to determine the constitutional issue which had been raised.

7.07 Although the point has not been directly decided,[13] it is unlikely that the power of a peace commissioner to receive a complaint and issue a summons continues to survive. The first indication of the weakness of his position is to be found in *State (Lynch) v. Ballagh*[14] where Walsh J, having noted the circumstances in which peace commissioners may remand an arrested person in custody or on bail, said that 'their position seems to be somewhat constitutionally dubious'. Although not expressing a view on

11 [1988] IR 470; [1988] ILRM 620.
12 At pp. 478-479 of the report.
13 It was raised in *Joyce v. Circuit Court Judge for the Western Circuit* [1987] ILRM 316 but not adjudicated upon.
14 [1986] IR 203, 212; [1987] ILRM 65.

the question of the constitutionality of the issue of a summons by a peace commissioner, Finlay CJ in *State (Clarke) v. Roche*[15] concluded that under section 10 of the Petty Sessions (Ireland) Act 1851 'the issue of a summons upon the making of a complaint was a judicial as distinct from an administrative act'. The chief justice then adverted to the judgment of Walsh J in *State (Lynch) v. Ballagh*.[16]

7.08 The complaint as the foundation of jurisdiction in summary proceedings 'To understand the importance and nature of the complaint it is necessary to advert shortly to the history of summary proceedings before Justices. Save for a few exceptional cases, of which this is not one, the jurisdiction of Justices to enter upon the hearing of an alleged offence, triable summarily, depended from the earliest times — and still depends — upon the making of a complaint or information before a person authorised to receive the complaint. . . . That an information or complaint to an authorised person is the very foundation of the jurisdiction hardly needs authority, but I may refer to *Paley on Convictions* (1st ed., 1814) at p. 14: "It is requisite in all summary proceedings that there should be an information or complaint, which is the basis of all subsequent proceedings and without which it seems that the Justice is not authorised in intermeddling." *Hutton on Convictions* (1st ed. 1835) has as the first words in his treatise: "In exercising the power of convicting summarily any person charged with having infringed the provisions of a statute the initiative proceeding is that the party complaining must present a statement of the offence complained of to a Justice authorised to take such an information." To the same effect are Nun and Walsh, *Justice of the Peace* (2nd ed., 1844), at p. 472; Molloy, *Justice of the Peace* (1890), at p. 169; O'Connor, *Justice of the Peace* (2nd ed., 1915), vol. 1, at p. 227. Neither summons nor warrant to arrest, consequent on the information, confer jurisdiction. They are merely processes to compel the attendance of the person accused of the offence: *R. (UDC of Athy) v. Justices of Kildare*; *R. v. Justices of Cork*. It is equally clear that if a person is in Court, voluntarily or involuntarily, legally or illegally, an information or complaint may be made then and there "ore tenus" to the Justice, accusing such person of having committed a summary offence, and, if the information contains the necessary ingredients, the person may at once be charged with the offence: *R. v. Fuller*; *R. v. Millard*; *Blake v. Beech*; *R. v. Hughes*; *R. v. Justices of Cork*.'[17]

15 [1986] IR 619, 641; [1987] ILRM 309.
16 Supra.
17 *Per* Kingsmill Moore J in *Attorney General (McDonnell) v. Higgins* [1964] IR 374, 390-391.

7.09 There is no form prescribed for the making of a complaint;[18] however, the District Court Rules provide that the recipient of a complaint may require it to be made on oath and in writing.[19] On the making of an information[20] or complaint, section 10 of the Petty Sessions (Ireland) Act 1851 provides that 'it shall be lawful for such Justice to receive such Information or Complaint, and to proceed in respect to the same'. According to O'Connor's *Justice of the Peace*:[21]

> It is well settled that a justice to whom an application is made for the issue of a summons . . . has a discretion, and if, in the proper exercise of that discretion he refuses to issue the summons . . . the High Court will not interfere. . . . What is meant by the proper exercise of discretion is that the justice must hear the application, and reasonably and judicially determine it, without misdirecting himself in law or allowing himself to be influenced by improper or extraneous consideration.

7.10 The time limit for the making of a complaint The Petty Sessions (Ireland) Act 1851[22] lays down a general time limit for the making of a complaint: it must be made 'within Six Months from the Time when the Cause of Complaint shall have arisen'. Two points should be noted in relation to this time limit: first, the six months refers to calendar months and, secondly, the day on which the offence has been committed is not taken into account.[23] In *Minister for Agriculture v. Norgro Ltd*[24] it was held that the question whether the time limit laid down by the Petty Sessions (Ireland) Act 1851 has been complied with is a matter of defence; so where the defendant contends that the complaint has not been made within the prescribed time, the prosecution should be permitted to prove the date of the complaint.

---

18 See *Irish Insurance Commissioners v. Trench* (1913) 47 ILTR 115 and see the judgment of Ó Dálaigh CJ in *Attorney General (McDonnell) v. Higgins* [1964] IR 374, 385.
19 DCR, 1948 r. 29.
20 An 'information' refers to a complaint made on oath and in writing.
21 Second edition, volume 1, p. 133.
22 Section 10, paragraph 4.
23 See O'Connor's *Justice of the Peace*, second edition, volume 1, p. 111. But see also the Interpretation Act 1937 section 11(h) which provides that, where time is computed from a particular day, that day should be included in the period. This section, however, only applies to the interpretation of an 'Act of the Oireachtas'.
24 [1980] IR 155. See also *State (Barr) v. McCay*, unreported judgment of the High Court (Doyle J) delivered 19 May 1980.

7.11 Indeed if the defence challenges the making of the complaint, the prosecution should prove by evidence that it has been properly made.[25] In *State (Byrne) v. Plunkett*[26] a computerised summons was issued bearing a date of complaint. In the course of cross-examination the defendant's counsel asked the complainant garda when he had, in fact, made the complaint. The garda was unable to give evidence of having communicated with the District Court clerk who received the complaint and stated that he had filled in a computer form requesting summonses probably on some date within six months of the alleged offence. The defendant's counsel then sought formal proof of the making of the complaint. The District Judge stated that he did not require proof that a complaint was made within six months of the alleged offence as the date on the summons was sufficient as evidence. He declined to allow the District Court clerk to be called to give evidence as to the making of the complaint and proceeded to convict the defendant. Making absolute a conditional order of certiorari, Darcy J held[27] that:

> to say that the six month time limit is a matter for Defence does not mean that it is a matter which Counsel for the Defence must seek to prove negatively and which the prosecution can ignore. The Prosecution must prove their Case. There are some Cases in which the prosecution must prove every aspect of their Case without being called upon to do so. There are some Cases such as this where it is open to the Defence to call on the Prosecution to prove something. It is clear that the fact that a complaint has been made or the date on which such complaint was made is a matter wholly within the knowledge of the Prosecution. An accused person could not possibly know when a complaint was made. To say that something is a matter for Defence means that it is a matter to be raised by the Defence. When the matter raised is a matter peculiarly in the knowledge of the Prosecution then it is up to the Prosecution to call evidence of that fact or matter. When this matter was raised by the Defendant's Counsel in the lower court I say firmly that the Prosecution should have proved it.

25 *Director of Public Prosecutions (Nagle) v. Flynn* [1987] IR 534 [1989] ILRM 65; *Director of Public Prosecutions v. Hussey*, unreported judgment of the High Court (Egan J) delivered 20 October 1987; *Duff v. Mangan* [1994] 1 ILRM 91; *Director of Public Prosecutions v. Maguire*, unwritten judgment of the High Court (Flood J) delivered 29 April 1994.

26 Unreported judgment of the High Court (Darcy J) delivered 1 July 1985. This case preceded *State (Clarke) v. Roche* [1986] IR 619 and later developments; see paras. 7.15-7.16 infra.

27 At p. 7 of the judgment.

7.12 The complaint and the summons These terms are often used interchangeably, but there is an important distinction between them which was succinctly explained by Henchy J in *Director of Public Prosecutions v. Gill*[28] when he pointed out that '... it is the complaint that gives jurisdiction and that the summons is merely a process to compel the attendance of the defendant in court'. In the *Director of Public Prosecutions v. Sheeran*[29] Gannon J, having reviewed the authorities, derived the following propositions from them. '(1) A complaint is a statement of facts constituting an offence. (2) Such a complaint is the initiative proceeding: it must be made to a person having authority to receive it. (3) Such person receiving the complaint must have authority to issue a summons and may do so. (4) The summons is a mere statement of the complaint notifying that a complaint has been made to an authorised person. (5) The summons of itself does not afford proof of the fact that a complaint was made. (6) Neither defect of form of a summons nor failure to serve or proceed on foot of it will invalidate the proceeding. (7) The court at which the person charged is present may proceed with a hearing notwithstanding deficiency in the form, contents or service of the summons. (8) The attendance of the person charged may be procured by the issue of a second summons issued by the same or a person other than one who has issued the first summons. (9) In the trial of an offence coming within s. 10(4) of the Petty Sessions (Ireland) Act 1851 it is a matter of proof that a complaint to an authorised person was made within six months from the commission of the offences alleged. (10) The issue of the summons and the making of the complaint need not be contemporaneous.'

7.13 Formal requirements The summons must direct the appearance of the defendant before a District Judge who has jurisdiction to hear and determine the complaint and at a court where the judge can exercise his jurisdiction.[30] It must also state the cause of the complaint.[31] Where an offence entails the doing or the omission to do any one of a number of different acts in the alternative, or an enactment states any part of an offence in the alternative, the acts, omissions or other matters stated in the alternative in the enactment may be stated either in the alternative or in the conjunctive in a summons.[32] In charging an offence contrary to statute it is sufficient to state the substance of the offence in ordinary language

---

28 [1980] IR 263, 267.
29 [1986] ILRM 579, 587-588.
30 DCR, 1948 r. 30(2).
31 DCR, 1948 r. 44.
32 Ibid.

with such particulars of the offence as may be necessary.³³ Two or more offences may be charged in the one summons.³⁴

7.14 The summons must be signed by the District Judge who issues it and may not be signed in blank.³⁵ In *State (O'Leary) v. Neilan*³⁶ the defendant sought an order of certiorari on the basis that the signature (in this case of the District Court clerk) had been affixed to the summons by the use of a rubber stamp and was not, in fact, a facsimile of the clerk's actual signature. The defendant's objection to the stamp was rejected because he had failed to make a clear and unequivocal challenge to it at various hearings of the case in the District Court and had, in fact, acquiesced in a number of adjournments. A copy of the summons must be issued for service on each defendant.³⁷

7.15 Summonses issued under the Courts (No. 3) Act 1986 The Courts (No. 3) Act 1986 provides a parallel procedure for the issue of summonses to that provided in the District Court Rules, 1948 and the Petty Sessions (Ireland) Act 1851. The enactment of the 1986 Act stemmed directly from the decision in *State (Clarke) v. Roche*³⁸ which concerned the consequences of the application of computerisation to the issue of summonses. In the High Court Barron J found that the procedure entailed the delivery to the office of the District Court clerk of a summons application form which was fed into a computer which printed out the appropriate form of summons. The signature of the clerk was then affixed to the summons either by the clerk or a duly authorised member of his staff. The defendant in the case objected that under this procedure the complaint grounding the issue of the summons could not be shown to have been considered by a person authorised to receive it. Upholding the objection, Barron J held³⁹ that 'it is quite clear that unless it can be shown that the District Court clerk has himself personally considered the complaints made, the jurisdiction of the court cannot have become exercisable and accordingly the summonses which have been issued are invalid'. Barron J's judgment was upheld by the Supreme Court. Finlay CJ, delivering the judgment of the court, held⁴⁰ that he could not 'accept

---

33 Ibid.
34 Ibid.
35 DCR, 1948 r. 45.
36 [1984] ILRM 35. As to the use of rubber stamp signatures see the judgment of Gavan Duffy P in *State (Attorney General) v. Roe* [1951] IR 172, 186-187.
37 DCR, 1948 r. 45.
38 [1986] IR 619; [1987] ILRM 309.
39 At p. 631 of the report.
40 At p. 641 of the report.

the proposition that . . . a complaint could be made to the District Court clerk without being communicated to him'. He held that 'the powers given to the Peace Commissioner and District Court Clerk to receive a complaint and issue a summons constituted the carrying out of a judicial act in a criminal matter'. But he went on[41] to express the view that 'it is no longer necessary or appropriate for a justice of the District Court or any other person to reach a judicial determination as to whether the summons should be issued'.

7.16 The legislature responded to the Supreme Court decision in *State (Clarke) v. Roche* with the enactment of the 1986 Act, the main features of which may be summarised as follows. The Act provides for the commencement of proceedings in the District Court in respect of an offence by issuing 'as a matter of administrative procedure' a document known as a summons.[42] The summons is to be issued under the general superintendence of an appropriate District Court clerk and must set out the name and address of the defendant and particulars of the offence alleged, and must notify the defendant that he will be accused of the offence at a specified sitting of the District Court.[43] The issue of the summons is to be procured by an application to the appropriate office of the District Court by or on behalf of a member of the Garda Síochána and certain others.[44] Lastly, the provisions of the Petty Sessions (Ireland) Act 1851[45] laying down a six month time limit for the making of a complaint apply to the application for a summons under the 1986 Act.[46]

7.17 **The validity of summonses issued under the 1986 Act** Following the enactment of the 1986 Act there was considerable confusion regarding the validity of summonses issued under its provisions. The principal problem stemmed from the fact that, when enacting the 1986 Act, the legislature did not repeal or amend section 10 of the Petty Sessions (Ireland) Act 1851 containing the requirement that a complaint be made within six months. Although this requirement remained on the statute book, it was not clear where it fitted into the scheme of things as laid down in the 1986 Act.[47] The problem was addressed by the Supreme Court in

---

41 Ibid.
42 Section 1(1) of the 1986 Act. The form of this summons is now prescribed in the District Court (Form of Summons) Rules, 1987, SI No. 23 of 1987.
43 Section 1(2) and (3) of the 1986 Act.
44 Section 1(4) of the 1986 Act.
45 See para. 7.10 supra.
46 Section 1(7)(a) of the 1986 Act.
47 Two decisions of the High Court after the enactment of the 1986 Act were contradictory. First, in the *Director of Public Prosecutions v. Shields* (unreported judgment of Gannon J deliv-

Director of Public Prosecutions v. Nolan and *Director of Public Prosecutions v. Roche and Kelly*.[48] Finlay CJ held that the effect of section 1(7)(a) of the 1986 Act was to substitute the date of the application for a summons for the date of the complaint for the purpose of the six month time limit laid down in the 1851 Act. In a summary at the end of his judgment[49] the chief justice stated his conclusions as follows. '(1) The Courts (No. 3) Act, 1986 duly authorises the issue of summonses for the trial of offences by the District Court. (2) The time limit applicable to summonses issued pursuant to the Act of 1986 is a limit of six months from the date of the alleged offence to the date of the application pursuant to section 1, subsection 4 for the issue of a summons. No other time limit arises except in the case of certain statutory offences where shorter time limits may apply. In the case of special shorter statutory time limits for summary offences, the time limit must be construed as being between the date of the offence and the date of the application for the summons. (3) The form of the summons provided for by the District Court (Form of Summons) Order, 1987 (SI No. 23), is adequate and proper for the purposes of the procedure provided by the Act of 1986. (4) A District Justice before whom

ered 4 December 1987) Gannon J, dealing with a summons issued under the 1986 Act, held that the District Judge should first have enquired whether the defendant was in court. If satisfied that he was not, the District Judge 'could then have heard the complaint and determined whether or not to issue a summons to procure (his) attendance'. If the defendant was in court, the District Judge had jurisdiction to 'hear in the presence of (the defendant) whatever complaint might be made and to determine what offence with which to charge (the defendant) and to decide whether or not to deal with those charges there and then or to require the attendance of (the defendant) for a hearing at another time' (p. 14 of the judgment). Gannon J held that the 1986 Act had 'set up a secondary mode of procedure whereby the issue of a summons can precede the making of a complaint' (p. 16 of the judgment). Shortly after *Director of Public Prosecutions v. Shields* Hamilton P (as he then was) gave judgment on similar issues in the case of *Director of Public Prosecutions v. Nolan* [1990] 2 IR 526. Here again summonses had been issued under the 1986 Act, but they were struck out by the District Judge who held that the complaints required by the Petty Sessions (Ireland) Act were made when made in court to him. On a case stated Hamilton P held that the judge had been wrong to strike out the summonses for that reason. The 1986 Act, he held, 'provides an additional method of invoking the jurisdiction of the District Court . . . and the learned District Justice erred in law in deciding that the making of a complaint in accordance with the provisions of the Petty Sessions (Ireland) Act 1851, was necessary to confer jurisdiction on him' (p. 538 of the report).

48 [1990] 2 IR 526; [1989] ILRM 39.
49 Pp. 546-547 of the report.

a person has been summoned pursuant to the provisions of the Act of 1986 is entitled, according to his or her discretion, upon it being satisfactorily established that such person was duly served with the summons but has not appeared, either to proceed to hear and determine the charge contained in the summons in the absence of the accused or, if he or she shall so decide, to adjourn the hearing of the summons to a later date and to secure the attendance of the accused by warrant or otherwise.' The effect, in short, of the Supreme Court decision is to uphold summonses issued under the 1986 Act, subject to the requirement that the application for the summons must generally be made within six months from the commission of the alleged offence. Where there was a doubt as to whether the application was made within the six month period because the summons was undated and no evidence was offered to show that it had been so made, the charge was held to have been rightly dismissed.[50]

7.18 Service In a drunken driving case the summons may be served by a member of the Garda Síochána or other person authorised by statute.[51] But a garda may not serve a summons in which he himself is the complainant.[52] The summons must be served at least seven clear days before the hearing of the complaint, unless served by registered post in which case service must be effected at least 21 days before the date fixed for the hearing.[53] It may be served on the defendant to whom it is directed by delivering to him a copy issued for service or by leaving the copy for him at his last or most usual place of abode or at his office, shop, factory, home or place of business with the husband or wife of the defendant or with a child or other relative (residing with the defendant) of the defendant himself or of his wife or her husband as the case may be, or with any agent, clerk or servant of the defendant, or with the person in charge of the house or premises wherein the defendant usually resides, provided that any person (other than the defendant himself) with whom the copy is left for the defendant is not under 16 years of age, and is not the complainant.[54] If

---

50 *Director of Public Prosecutions v. Maguire*, unwritten judgment of the High Court (Flood J) delivered 29 April 1994.
51 See DCR, 1948 r. 46(1)(a) as substituted by the District Court Rules (No. 1), 1962, SI No. 7 of 1962.
52 See DCR, 1948 r. 46(1)(c) as substituted by the District Court Rules (No. 1), 1962, SI No. 7 of 1962.
53 See DCR, 1948 r. 47(1)(a) as substituted by the District Court Rules (No. 1), 1962, SI No. 7 of 1962. See *Le Gear v. Mangan*, unreported judgment of the High Court (Barron J) delivered 16 December 1994, a case where seven clear days' notice was not given.
54 See DCR, 1948 r. 47(2)(a) as substituted by the District Court Rules (No. 1), 1962, SI No. 7 of 1962.

none of these modes of service is reasonably practicable, the District Judge may direct that service be effected in such manner as he thinks proper.[55] Section 22 of the Courts Act 1991 allows for the service of summonses in cases of summary jurisdiction by registered post. The section authorises service by sending a copy of the summons by registered prepaid post in an envelope addressed to the person to whom it is directed at his last known residence or most usual place of abode or at his place of business.

7.19 The person who serves a summons must prove service either by giving evidence orally and upon oath before the District Judge in court or by making a statutory declaration of service before a judge or peace commissioner endorsed upon the back of the original summons.[56] The statutory declaration is prima facie evidence of the mode, time and place of service but the judge may require the person who effected service to attend and give evidence on oath touching the service.[57] Time for the service or lodgment of a summons may be extended or abridged by the judge whenever he thinks fit.[58]

7.20 Reissued summonses Suppose a complaint or application is made and a summons is issued but for whatever reason is not served, and that a further summons is then issued outside the six month time limit laid down in the Petty Sessions (Ireland) Act 1851. Is this 'reissued' summons valid or, more accurately, has the court jurisdiction to determine the charge set out in it? The answer is that it has whether the summons is an old type summons issued under the Petty Sessions (Ireland) Act 1851 or a new type issued under the Courts (No. 3) Act 1986 so long as the issue of the new summons was founded on the original complaint. Thus in *Director of Public Prosecutions v. Gill*[59] Henchy J held that: 'If the complaint on which the fresh summons is founded was made within the six months following on the time when the cause of complaint arose, it matters not that the fresh summons was issued after the expiration of the six months period.' More recently in *Director of Public Prosecutions v. McKillen*[60] the question was considered in the context of summonses issued under the 1986 Act. Here a summons had been issued on 3 August 1989, but on account of difficulties

---

55 See DCR, 1948 r. 47(2)(c) as substituted by the District Court Rules (No. 1), 1962, SI No. 7 of 1962.
56 DCR, 1948 r. 49.
57 Ibid.
58 DCR, 1948 r. 51(1).

59 [1980] IR 263, 267-268. See also *Director of Public Prosecutions v. Sheeran* [1986] ILRM 579 and *State (Gartlan) v. O'Donnell* [1986] ILRM 588.
60 [1991] 2 IR 508.

in serving the defendant a second summons was issued on 27 September 1989. The first summons had been issued within the six month time limit, but the second had not. The nett issue, according to Lavan J,[61] was whether 'a summons properly issued under the Act of 1986 within the six month period can be re-issued outside of the period of six months'. He held that it could and that[62] 'having regard to the right under the procedure as laid down by the Act of 1851 (ie the Petty Sessions (Ireland) Act) to re-issue a summons grounded on the original complaint it seems . . . clear that such a right is not only consistent but must be read as being one of the "any necessary modifications" referred to in section 1 subsection 7(a) of the Act of 1986'.

PROCEDURE BY CHARGE SHEET

7.21 A drunken driving prosecution may also be initiated by charging the defendant on a charge sheet. This procedure is regulated by the District Court (Charge Sheet) Rules, 1971.[63] It may be used whenever a person is arrested and brought to a garda station or where an offence is alleged against a person who is already on remand to the District Court and a summons in respect of the offence is not issued.[64] Particulars of the offence must be set out on the charge sheet which must be in accordance with the prescribed form or such modification as may be suitable.[65] A copy of the particulars must be furnished as soon as may be to the person against whom the offence is alleged.[66] The sheet must be lodged as soon as possible with the District Court clerk for the District Court area in which the case is to be heard.[67]

7.22 Following the charging of the accused on a charge sheet he must be brought before a District Judge.[68] Section 15(2) of the Criminal Justice Act 1951 as substituted by section 26 of the Criminal Justice Act 1984 provides that: 'A person arrested without warrant shall, on being charged with an offence, be brought before a justice of the District Court having jurisdiction to deal with the offence or, if a justice is not immediately

---

61 At p. 510 of the report.
62 At p. 512 of the report.
63 SI No. 225 of 1971.
64 District Court (Charge Sheet) Rules, 1971 r. 3(1).
65 Ibid.
66 District Court (Charge Sheet) Rules, 1971 r. 3(2).
67 District Court (Charge Sheet) Rules, 1971 r. 3(3).
68 See the judgment of Walsh J in *State (Lynch) v. Ballagh* [1986] IR 203; [1987] ILRM 65.

available, before a peace commissioner in the district of such a justice as soon as practicable.'[69] In addition, section 15(4) of the 1951 Act as substituted by section 26 of the 1984 Act purported to empower a peace commissioner to remand the person, either in custody or on bail, and to remit the case for hearing before a judge of the District Court; but in *O'Mahony v. Melia*[70] it was held that the exercise of this power constituted a judicial act from which a peace commissioner is precluded under the provisions of the Constitution. If, on being brought before a District Judge, bail is fixed and the accused finds bail, the case must be remitted to the next sitting of the court.[71] Otherwise the case must be remitted to a sitting of the court at a named place to be held within eight days after the arrest.[72] A person charged in a garda station may also be released on admission to station bail. Thus section 31(1) of the Criminal Procedure Act 1967 provides that the sergeant or other member in charge of the station may release the person on bail and take from him a recognizance, with or without sureties, for his due appearance before the District Court at the appropriate time and place. On foot of the decision of the Supreme Court in *State (Lynch) v. Ballagh*[73] and that of the High Court in *Maguire v. Shelly*[74] it is clear that the person released may be bound by the recognizance to appear at the next sitting of the District Court in the court area in which the arrest took place.

7.23 The use of the charge sheet procedure does not dispense with the need for a complaint as the foundation for the exercise of jurisdiction by the District Court. This point was clearly made by Kingsmill Moore J in *Attorney General (McDonnell) v. Higgins*.[75] In that case the accused was charged on a charge sheet in a garda station. He was subsequently brought before the District Court and numerous remands were granted. Referring to the charging of the accused in the garda station, Kingsmill Moore J held:[76]

---

69 Where the charge is made after 10 o'clock in the evening, and a judge is due to sit in the District Court district in which the person has been arrested not later than noon on the following day, it is sufficient if he is brought before the judge at the commencement of the sitting: section 15(3) of the Criminal Justice Act 1951 as substituted by section 26 of the Criminal Justice Act 1984.

70 [1989] IR 335; [1990] ILRM 14.

71 Section 15(5) of the Criminal Justice Act 1951 as substituted by section 26 of the Criminal Justice Act 1984.

72 Section 15(6) of the Criminal Justice Act 1951 as substituted by section 26 of the Criminal Justice Act 1984.

73 [1986] IR 203; [1987] ILRM 65.

74 [1992] 1 IR 482.

75 [1964] IR 374.

76 At p. 393 of the report. See also the judgment of Ó Dálaigh CJ at p. 385.

This charge cannot be a complaint or information for it is not made before a District Justice, a Peace Commissioner or a Clerk. The charge sheet on which it is entered initiates as a purely police document and the entry of the offences charged is necessary for the protection of the garda to show that such offences justify arrest and detention in the barracks without warrant. Subsequently, when the charge sheet is put before the District Justice and the final two columns are utilised by him to record his decisions, it becomes a document of the Court, but before the District Justice enters on the case it seems to me that there must be a complaint to him by some person, preferably but not necessarily the Superintendent, alleging the commission of the offences by the defendant with such particularity and details as are required by the authorities for a legal complaint. Only when this has been done is jurisdiction conferred to enter on the hearing of the case.

Notwithstanding these dicta, it would now seem to be accepted that the complaint is made when the charge sheet is put before the District Judge.[77]

DELAY

7.24 It is well established that delay in the prosecution of an offence resulting in prejudice to the defendant may bar a conviction. According to Henchy J in *Director of Public Prosecutions v. Gill*,[78] 'If . . . because of undue delay in issuing the summons or in bringing it to a hearing, the defendant is unfairly prejudiced in making his defence, natural justice may require that the summons be dismissed.' Much more problematic has been the question whether delay, without evidence of specific prejudice, may be a bar. The answer is that in certain circumstances it may, and delay is a bar when it results in an infringement of the defendant's constitutional right to a trial with reasonable expedition.[79] After a series of cases in the High Court[80] the issue was authoritatively considered by the Supreme

---

77 See the judgment of Walsh J in *State (Lynch) v. Ballagh* [1986] IR 203 [1987] ILRM 65 and *Director of Public Prosecutions (Nagle) v. Flynn* [1987] IR 534 [1989] ILRM 65.

78 [1980] IR 263, 268.

79 *State (O'Connell) v. Fawsitt* [1986] IR 362; [1986] ILRM 639.

80 *State (Cuddy) v. Mangan* [1988] ILRM 720; *Maher v. Carroll*, unreported judgment of the High Court (Blayney J) delivered 8 August 1986; *Director of Public Prosecutions v. Burnby*, unreported judgment of the High Court (Barr J) delivered 24 July 1989; *Director of Public Prosecutions v. Carlton* [1993] 1 IR 81; *Director of Public Prosecutions v. Bouchier Hayes*,

Court in *Director of Public Prosecutions v. Byrne*[81] which concerned an offence of drunken driving alleged to have occurred on 19 April 1991. The prosecuting garda applied for a summons on 27 May 1991 which did not issue until 19 December 1991. It was served shortly thereafter and the matter came on for hearing in the District Court on 12 February 1992. The District Judge held that there had been an unreasonable delay for which the prosecution had offered no adequate explanation and dismissed the charge. On a case stated to the High Court it was held that she had been correct in dismissing the charge, but this decision was reversed by a three to two majority on appeal to the Supreme Court. Blayney J, with whose judgment O'Flaherty J agreed, adverted[82] to 'the difficult question of determining when a delay or lapse of time is excessive' and held that 'no clear rule can be laid down in regard to this. It will depend on the particular circumstances of each case. Matters to be taken into account would include the nature of the offence, the cause of the delay and the possibility that the defence will be impaired. . . .' In the circumstances of the case Blayney J thought there had been no unreasonable delay. Denham J, the third member of the majority and with whose judgment O'Flaherty J also agreed, agreed that the delay in the case (not quite ten months) was not unreasonable, and held that in the absence of evidence of prejudice no constitutional right of the defendant had been infringed. She said that the question whether a defendant's right to reasonable expedition has been infringed can be determined only on an ad hoc basis and suggested that a court should have regard to the four factors identified by the Supreme Court of the United States in *Barker v. Wingo*:[83] length of the delay, the reason for the delay, the defendant's assertion of his right and prejudice to the defendant. The *Byrne* decision does not preclude the dismissal of a charge on the ground of excessive delay. But it does establish (presumably as a general proposition) that the prosecution is not bound to explain or justify a delay and that, in a drunken driving prosecution, a delay of under ten months does not of itself infringe a defendant's right to reasonable expedition so as to bar a court from proceeding to conviction.

unreported judgment of the High Court (Carroll J) delivered 19 December 1992; and *Director of Public Prosecutions v. Corbett (No. 1)* [1991] 2 IR 1 and *Director of Public Prosecutions v. Corbett (No. 2)* [1992] ILRM 674 (the No. 2 Corbett judgment was appealed to the Supreme Court which in ex tempore judgments delivered on 16 October 1992 upheld the judgment of the High Court).

81 [1994] 2 IR 236.
82 At p. 253 of the report.
83 (1972) 407 US 514.

8

The Hearing

8.01 The hearing of cases of summary jurisdiction is dealt with in rule 64 of the District Court Rules.[1] The substance of the complaint should be stated to the defendant or his legal representative.[2] If the defendant admits the truth of the complaint, the District Judge may, if he sees no sufficient reason to the contrary, convict or make an order against him.[3] But if he does not admit the truth of the complaint, the judge must proceed to hear and determine the complaint.[4] He may also proceed where the defendant or his legal representative has not appeared and the summons has been duly served.[5]

---

[1] And in section 20 of the Petty Sessions (Ireland) Act 1851. Many provisions in the District Court Rules have been adapted from the Petty Sessions (Ireland) Act 1851, most of which has never been repealed. This led to the following observations of Gavan Duffy P in 1949 in *State (Attorney General) v. Roe* [1951] IR 172, 180-181: 'A surprising and, I think, unforeseen result of the statutory power to make rules was the emergence in the year 1926 of an elaborate code of rules for the District Court, a code which, besides making some amendments, reproduced in large part the existing provisions of the Act of 1851, without repealing them. The result was that the new rules jostled the statute at every turn and, if the District Court proved to be a conspicuous success during its first twenty-four years, that success was achieved despite the clumsy experiment at a most unscientific dichotomous code.'

[2] DCR, 1948 r. 64(1).

[3] Ibid. In *State (McCann) v. Wine* [1981] IR 134 it was held that a plea of guilty should not be accepted before the substance of the complaint has been stated to the defendant; and that the existence of a complaint charging a serious indictable offence under section 53 of the Road Traffic Act 1961 is a 'sufficient reason to the contrary' to enable a District Judge to exercise his discretion to refrain from convicting the defendant of careless driving and so precluding the prosecution from proceeding with the serious indictable offence.

[4] Ibid.

[5] Or he may, in such circumstances, issue a warrant for the defendant's arrest: DCR, 1948 r. 64(2) and see DCR, 1948 rr. 40 and 41. If the complainant does not appear and the defendant or his legal representative has appeared, the District Judge may dismiss the complaint either without

8.02 Hearing and determining the complaint When a District Judge proceeds to hear and determine a complaint, he must, if required to do so by either party or by the legal representative for such party, take or cause to be taken a note in writing of the evidence or so much of the evidence as is material.[6] Apart from this formal requirement, the judge has a more fundamental obligation to ensure that the trial is conducted, as required by article 38(1) of the Constitution, 'in due course of law'. It is well established that 'due course of law' necessitates the application of fair procedures and that the accused be afforded an adequate opportunity to defend himself.[7] More specifically, it has been said[8] that: 'Among the natural rights of an individual whose conduct is impugned and whose freedom is put in jeopardy are the rights to be adequately informed of the nature and substance of the accusation, to have the matter tried in his presence by an impartial and independent court or arbitrator, to hear and test by examination the evidence offered by or on behalf of his accuser, to be allowed to give or call evidence in his defence, and to be heard in argument or submission before judgment is given.' But this is not an exhaustive statement of the rights of an accused; the judge stressed[9] that: 'By mentioning these (rights) I am not to be taken as giving a complete summary, or as excluding other rights such as the right to reasonable expedition or the right to have an opportunity for preparation of the defence.'

8.03 In the conduct of the trial the trial judge must permit the defendant or his legal representative to ask all and any relevant questions he may seek to ask;[10] he must allow relevant submissions on the law to be made;[11] he

---

  prejudice to its being made again or on the merits or he may adjourn the hearing: DCR, 1948 r. 64(3).

6 DCR, 1948 r. 64(5) which provides that the note is to be made in a book kept for that purpose by the clerk and that the book must be signed by the judge by whom the information or complaint has been heard on the day on which it is determined; see also section 20(4) of the Petty Sessions (Ireland) Act 1851. But if a District Judge fails to keep a note this will not invalidate an order made by him: *Hegarty v. Fitzpatrick* [1990] 2 IR 377. Nor will an order be invalidated if he has kept a note and refuses to furnish it to the defendant: *Friel v. McMenamin* [1990] 2 IR 210; [1990] ILRM 761.

7 See Kelly, *The Irish Constitution* (Dublin, 1994), third edition, pp. 572-603 and pp. 614-619.

8 By Gannon J in *State (Healy) v. Donoghue* [1976] IR 325, 335-336.

9 Ibid. at p. 336.

10 *Gill v. Connellan* [1987] IR 541 [1988] ILRM 448; *O'Broin v. Ruane* [1989] IR 214.

11 *McNally v. Martin*, unreported judgment of the High Court (Murphy J) delivered 14 January 1994.

is not entitled to require the defendant to give evidence or to call a witness;[12] and he may in an appropriate case allow the prosecution to reopen its case, but not in circumstances where the defendant is deprived of representation by the lawyer of his choice.[13] Above all, the trial judge must ensure that the defendant receives a fair trial, a point illustrated by *Gill v. Connellan*[14] where the defendant was charged with a drunken driving offence. In the District Court his solicitor cross-examined the arresting garda as to the manner in which the blood sample had been taken, suggesting that the garda had squeezed the defendant's arm to enable the doctor to take blood from it. During the course of this cross-examination the trial judge intervened to enquire as to its relevance. The solicitor said that he was trying to establish that the proper procedure had not been complied with for taking the sample whereupon the judge said: 'It does not matter what you say, the Act was complied with.' When the solicitor submitted that the sample had not been obtained in the usual or proper manner, the judge replied: 'You are wasting time.' The solicitor submitted that he was entitled to make his argument to which the judge replied: 'You can go on and on for all the good it will do you. I am not interested in it.' The solicitor read an extract from the first edition of this book[15] which the judge again interrupted. He submitted that the manner in which the sample had been taken was illegal as it involved a technical assault to which the judge said: 'I do not care: I am not interested: Do you want to call any witnesses?' In view of the judge's attitude the solicitor decided there was no point in calling witnesses. The judge convicted and the defendant sought judicial review by way of certiorari which was granted. In another case the proper purpose of intervention by the trial judge was described thus by McCarthy J in his characteristic trenchant style:[16]

> The role of the trial judge in maintaining an even balance will require that on occasion he must intervene in the questioning of witnesses with questions of his own — the purpose being to clarify the unclear, to complete the incomplete, to elaborate the inadequate and to truncate the long-winded. It is not to embellish, to emphasise or, save rarely, to criticise. That is the function of counsel.

12 *State (O'Connor) v. Larkin* [1968] IR 255; *Singh v. Ruane* [1989] IR 610.
13 *Dawson v. Hamill* [1989] IR 275; [1990] ILRM 257.
14 [1987] IR 541; [1988] ILRM 448. See also *State (O'Reilly) v. Windle*, unreported judgment of the High Court (Blayney J) delivered 4 November 1986; *Sweeney v. Brophy* [1993] 2 IR 202; *Dineen v. Delap* [1994] 2 IR 228.
15 P. 40 of that edition where the judgment of O'Higgins CJ in *Director of Public Prosecutions v. Kemmy* [1980] IR 160 is quoted.
16 *Donnelly v. Timber Factors Ltd* [1991] 1 IR 553 (a personal injury action).

8.04 Advance notice of the evidence In *Cowzer v. Kirby*[17] it was held that constitutional justice and fair procedures require that a person charged with an indictable offence, who elects to be tried summarily, be furnished prior to his trial with copies of the statements of witnesses whose evidence is crucial to the case against him. Following the *Cowzer* decision it became a frequent practice for the prosecution, even in the case of summary offences such as drunken driving, to make available, when sought by a defendant, copies of statements made by its witnesses. The question whether the prosecution was obliged to furnish statements was reconsidered in *Director of Public Prosecutions v. Doyle*[18] which again concerned an indictable offence tried summarily. Geoghegan J followed the earlier decision in *Clune v. Director of Public Prosecutions*[19] and held that there is no general obligation, but qualified his judgment with the observation[20] that 'the Constitution guarantees fair procedures in all trials whether summary or upon indictment. Therefore, if in any given case fair procedures dictate that an accused in a summary trial should be given advance notice of the material evidence against him, then the Judge should not embark on the trial unless that is done.' On appeal the Supreme Court affirmed that there is no general obligation to furnish the prosecution statements, but like Geoghegan J the court recognised that there may be cases where fair procedures require that copies of the statements be furnished. The question falls to be determined by the District Judge by reference to 'the interests of justice'. Among the matters to be considered, according to the Supreme Court, are (1) the seriousness of the charge, (2) the importance of the statements, (3) whether the accused has already been adequately informed of the nature and substance of the accusation and (4) the risk of injustice.

8.05 Variances, defects, omissions and the power to amend Variances, defects and omissions are dealt with in rule 88 of the District Court Rules. No variance between the complaint and the evidence adduced in support of it, as to the time at which the offence or cause of complaint is stated to have been committed or to have arisen, is to be deemed material, provided that the information or complaint was made within the time limited by law.[21] Nor is a variance as to the place in which the offence or cause of complaint is stated to have been committed or to have arisen to

---

17 Unreported judgment of the High Court (Barr J) delivered 11 February 1991.
18 [1994] 2 IR 286; [1994] 1 ILRM 529.
19 [1981] ILRM 17.
20 At p. 292 of the report.
21 DCR, 1948 r. 88(1).

be deemed material, provided that the offence or cause of complaint was committed or arose within the jurisdiction of the judge by whom the case is being heard or the defendant resides or was arrested within that jurisdiction.[22] The judge may amend the summons or other document by which the proceedings were originated and proceed to hear and determine the matter.[23] The District Judge is also empowered to amend or proceed as though no defect exists where objection is taken on the ground of a defect in substance or in form or of an omission in the summons or other document by which the proceedings were initiated, or of any variance between such document and the evidence adduced on the part of the complainant at the hearing of the case.[24] But where, in his opinion, the variance, defect or omission is one which has misled or prejudiced the defendant or which might affect the merits of the case, he may refuse to make any amendment and dismiss the complaint either without prejudice to its being made again or on the merits.[25] If he makes an amendment, he may adjourn the proceedings upon such terms as he thinks fit.[26] The amendment may be made whether the defendant does or does not appear at the hearing at which the variance, defect or omission comes to the notice of the judge, provided the defendant was duly served with a summons or bound by recognizance to appear at the hearing.[27]

8.06   The foregoing provisions of rule 88 were considered *Director of Public Prosecutions v. Winston*.[28] Here the defendant was charged with a drunken driving offence at 'Tawnaghmore, Cummer in the County of Galway', but the evidence was that he had been stopped and arrested in the townland of Cummer, and not in Tawnaghmore which was an adjoining but separate townland. The District Judge acquitted but on appeal by case stated to the High Court it was held the matter should be remitted to the District Court. Referring to rule 88, O'Hanlon J held[29] that:

> these provisions in the District Court Rules were designed to discourage the taking of purely technical objections based on vari-

22   Ibid.
23   Ibid. A District Judge also has power to amend under rule 21 of the District Court Rules which provides that he may amend a summons or other proceeding by adding or striking out parties and may amend such other defects and errors as may be necessary for the purpose of determining the real question at issue between the parties.
24   DCR, 1948 r. 88(2).
25   DCR, 1948 r. 88(3).
26   Ibid.
27   DCR, 1948 r. 88(4).
28   Unreported judgment of the High Court (O'Hanlon J) delivered 25 May 1992.
29   At pp. 3-4 of the judgment.

ations between the written detail of the complaint and the facts established in evidence and to leave scope for the District Judge to resolve such matters of objection by amendment, if necessary on his or her own motion without awaiting a formal application for an amendment on the part of the prosecution. I am also of opinion that the Rules envisage that this course will be taken by the Judge except when it appears to him or her that the variance, defect or omission is one which has misled or prejudiced the Defendant or which might affect the merits of the case. Even if he or she does form such opinion, the position of the accused person can be protected either by making the amendment subject to adjourning the proceedings to a later date, or by dismissing without prejudice to the complaint being again made, and it appears to me that a dismiss on the merits based on a purely technical objection to the form of the complaint should be very much the exception rather than the rule.

8.07 The power to amend The principles upon which a District Judge should exercise his discretion to amend were laid down by Finlay P (as he then was) in *State (Duggan) v. Evans*[30] where he held that: ' If . . . a District Justice concludes that there is a defect in substance or form or an omission in the document by which a prosecution before him has been originated or that there is a variance between it and the evidence adduced for the prosecution, he is bound to proceed as follows: 1. He must first ascertain as to whether the variance, defect or omission has in his opinion misled or prejudiced the defendant or might in his opinion affect the merits of the case. 2. If he is of opinion that none of these consequences has occurred he must either amend the document or proceed as if no such defect, variance, or omission had existed . . . Where, as would appear to the position in this case, amendment is necessary to make a conviction on the charge valid, the amendment should be made; where it is not it may be omitted. Furthermore, this jurisdiction and obligation of the Justice in an appropriate case to make an amendment is not in my view dependent on an application by the prosecution but can and should be exercised, as is the power of a Court to amend an Indictment, on his own initiative. 3. If on the other hand the Justice is of the opinion that the frailty in the document has misled or prejudiced the defendant or if of the opinion that it might affect the merits of the case three alternative courses are open to him: (a) he may dismiss the case without prejudice, (b) he may dismiss

---

30 (1978) 112 ILTR 61, 63.

the case on the merits, (c) he may amend the document and adjourn the case upon terms. Again the Rule (rule 88) contains no express guidance as to the grounds on which the choice between these three alternatives must be made and it is not possible to define them with particularity save that the decision must presumably rest on the extent and nature of the misleading, prejudice, or possible affect on the merits of the case set against the requirements of justice between the prosecution and the defendant. It would appear to me that a dismiss on the merits would not appear to be justified unless the opinion of the Justice was that there was a possibility that the defect would affect the merits in a manner not certain to be cured by adjournment or that an adjournment was necessary but would be an injustice.' These principles were recently applied in *Director of Public Prosecutions v. Corbett*[31] where the prosecution sought to amend summonses, including a summons alleging a drunken driving offence, so as to change the address of the defendant from '27 Coolmine Boulevard' to '25 Coolmine Boulevard' and the date of the alleged offence from '19 September 1989' to '18 September 1989'. The defendant contended that he was prejudiced by the latter amendment as he had brought alibi witnesses to court in respect of the date charged in the summons. The District Judge refused the application to amend and dismissed the summonses. On a case stated to the High Court it was held that, when considering the proposed amendments, the District Judge had to ascertain whether they misled or prejudiced the defendant or might affect the merits of the case; the matter was, on that basis, remitted to the District to reconsider the application to amend. On this occasion the District Judge amended the summonses other than the drunken driving summons which he dismissed. A second case stated resulted in Lynch J holding that the drunken driving summons should also have been amended, a decision which was upheld on appeal to the Supreme Court.

8.08 The power of the District Judge to amend was also considered in *Attorney General (McDonnell) v. Higgins*.[32] Here the defendant was charged on a charge sheet with road traffic offences. The charge sheet did not refer to the statute nor were the words 'against the statute in such case made and provided' included in it. After numerous remands, an application was made to amend the charge sheet by including the words 'contrary to the statute in such case made and provided' at the end of the charges. It was

31 [1991] 2 IR 1 and [1992] ILRM 674 which was upheld on appeal to the Supreme Court, judgments delivered 16 October 1992.
32 [1964] IR 374.

held that the omission of a reference to the statute comes within the ambit of rule 88 of the District Court Rules, 1948 and that by amending the charge the District Judge would not be substituting a new complaint for the original complaint.

8.09 The power to adjourn A District Judge may at any stage adjourn a case to such day and place as he thinks fit.[33] On granting an adjournment he may allow the defendant to go at large or may remand him on bail or in custody to appear at the time and place to which the hearing has been adjourned, but no remand in custody may be for a period exceeding eight clear days.[34] The discretion to adjourn must be exercised judicially, and so long as it is properly exercised the superior courts will not interfere.[35] The discretion was considered in the context of a drunken driving charge brought under under the provisions of section 49 of the Road Traffic Act 1961 as amended by the Road Traffic Act 1968 in *Verdon v. Downes*.[36] At the outset of the hearing the solicitor for the prosecution indicated that he might seek an adjournment in order to procure the attendance of a witness from the Bureau of Road Safety to prove a certificate. However, he closed his case without calling the witness nor seeking an adjournment for that purpose. After counsel for the defendant sought to have the case dismissed, he then requested the adjournment which was refused. The Supreme Court held that the District Judge, having exercised his discretion, was correct in dismissing the complaint. A prosecution request for an adjournment was also refused in *Director of Public Prosecutions v. Fahy*[37] where the adjournment sought was for an indefinite period pending the determination of an appeal from the High Court to the Supreme Court. District Judge Brennan held that such an adjournment would be a denial of justice to the defendant.

8.10 Non-compliance with the District Court Rules The District Court Rules provide that non-compliance with any of the Rules does not

---

33 DCR, 1948 r. 64(4) as amended by the District Court Rules (No. 3), 1948, SI No. 431 of 1948, and as amended by the District Court Rules, 1955, SI No. 83 of 1955; see also Courts of Justice Act 1953 section 27(3).
34 Ibid.
35 *State (Attorney General) v. Mangan* [1961] Ir Jur Rep 17; *State (Llewellyn) v. Ua Donnchadha* [1973] IR 151. But see *Butler v. Ruane*, unreported judgment of the High Court (Carroll J) delivered 21 July 1988; *Flynn v. Ruane* [1989] ILRM 690; *Grennan v. Kirby* [1994] 2 ILRM 199 (cases where the High Court did interfere).
36 Unreported decision of the Supreme Court, judgment delivered 29 July 1976.
37 (1987) 5 ILT (NS) 270.

render render proceedings void.[38] But in case of non-compliance, a District Judge may direct that the proceedings be treated as void, or that they be set aside in part as irregular, or that they be amended or otherwise dealt with as he thinks fit.[39] The District Judge must cause a note of any such ruling to be made in the appropriate book.[40]

8.11 The adjudication other than conviction[41] A District Judge who does not convict may dismiss a complaint either on the merits or without prejudice to its being made again.[42] A dismiss on the merits is a bar to a second charge for the same offence, whereas a dismiss without prejudice is not.[43] In *Morris v. Long*[44] it was held that an order of dismiss without prejudice should be confined to cases where there has been a failure to prove the complainant's case arising from some oversight in regard to a technical proof and where the judge thinks that, in the circumstances, fresh proceedings should be brought. Since the decision of the High Court in *State (Clarke) v. Roche*[45] there is a question whether, following an order of dismiss without prejudice, a second complaint must be made grounding the issue of a fresh summons. The judgment of Barron J suggests that there is no need for a further complaint, and that a second prosecution may be brought based on the complaint which has been so dismissed. These remarks are, however, probably obiter and certainly seem to conflict with the plain wording of the relevant rule.[46]

8.12 Another course open to a District Judge is to strike out a complaint, but there is authority that where the prosecution press the charge the judge should determine it and either convict or dismiss.[47] The order of strike out is appropriate where the provisions of the District Court Rules have

---

38 DCR, 1948 r. 23.
39 Ibid.
40 Ibid.
41 See generally Woods, *District Court Practice and Procedure in Criminal Cases* (Limerick, 1994), chapter 8.
42 DCR, 1948 r. 66.
43 *Attorney General (O'Gara) v. Callanan* (1958) 52 ILTR 74.
44 [1955-6] Ir Jur Rep 13.
45 [1986] IR 619; [1987] ILRM 309.
46 Rule 66 of DCR, 1948—and indeed with the corresponding provision in the Petty Sessions Ireland Act 1851, section 21 which, inter alia, requires that 'One of the Justices . . . enter or cause the Clerk to enter Particulars of (the) Case and the Substance of the Decision thereon in a Book to be kept for that Purpose, to be called the 'Order Book' . . . and shall, in case of a Dismissal, state whether the same is upon the Merits or without Prejudice *to a further Complaint . . .*' (author's emphasis). Section 21 of the 1851 Act has, however, been repealed by section 26 and the second schedule to the Criminal Justice Act 1951.
47 *Attorney General v. Mallen* [1957] IR 344.

not been complied with, or where the judge is of the opinion that the complaint discloses no offence at law, or if neither party appears.[48] The District Court Rules provide[49] that such an order will not debar fresh proceedings in the same matter. Whether a fresh complaint is required is not clear. But if a complaint has been struck out because it discloses no offence at law, then certainly, as Barron J pointed out in *State (Clarke) v. Roche*,[50] there must be a second complaint.

8.13 If no order is made in respect of a summons when it comes on for hearing, it may be held to have lapsed. Thus in *Director of Public Prosecutions v. Gill*[51] two sets of summonses were issued against the defendant in respect of the same offences. When the first set came on for hearing there was no appearance by the complainant and the District Judge made no order on the summonses. When the second set came on for hearing a point was raised by the defendant's solicitor under the Petty Sessions (Ireland) Act 1851. A case was stated to the High Court and, on appeal to the Supreme Court, it was held that, since no order had been made on the first set of summonses, they had lapsed and that fresh summonses could be issued in respect of the same complaint. The District Judge was held to be entitled to hear and determine the fresh summonses but, more properly, the first summonses should have been struck out beforehand.

8.14 The conviction 'The fundamental requirements of a good order on conviction are,' according to Finlay P (as he then was) in *State (Sugg) v. O'Sullivan*,[52] 'that it will set out in clear and unambiguous terms the precise offence by reference to statute in the case of a statutory offence and by reference to an acceptable common law definition in the case of a common law offence of which the accused was found guilty and that furthermore it will contain such material facts as will identify the manner in which the offence was committed, the date upon which it was committed and the place where it was committed so as to prevent in effect the person so convicted from ever being charged with the same offence again and so as to leave him with a record of the matter in respect of which he was convicted on which he could safely ground a plea of autre fois convict were he ever to be charged with the same offence again.' The requirements of

---

48 DCR, 1948 r. 66. It is also the appropriate order when the judge considers that he does not have jurisdiction to deal with the matter before him: *Carpenter v. Kirby* [1990] ILRM 764.

49 Ibid.
50 Supra.
51 [1980] IR 263.
52 Unreported judgment of the High Court delivered 23 June 1980.

a good conviction are summarised in O'Connor's *Justice of the Peace*[53] as follows:

> (1) that it be full and correct; (2) that the directions of the particular statute relative to the offence should appear on the face of the conviction to have been substantially complied with, both as regards the subject matter of the offence being clearly brought within the statute, and the adjudication; (3) that it be certain; (4) that all the facts necessary to support a conviction must be expressly alleged and not left to be gathered by inference or intendment. . . . Proceeding to deal with the particular contents of a conviction, every conviction must contain: (1) a statement showing that the offence is within the jurisdiction, (2) names of complainant and defendant, (3) time of offence, (4) place of offence, (5) description of offence with certainty and accuracy, (6) an adjudication permitted by statute.

In addition, the Supreme Court has held that a conviction for a statutory offence must show that the offence was statutory either by referring to a particular statute and section or by using the formula 'contrary to the statute in such case made and provided'.[54]

8.15 Of these requirements the requirement of certainty in a conviction has not infrequently led to convictions for driving offences being held open to challenge. Certainty in a conviction requires that the offence be fully and accurately stated. So, for example, in *Butler v. Mahon*[55] a conviction contrary to section 13(3) of the Road Traffic (Amendment) Act 1978 that the defendant did 'forthwith' fail to comply with a requirement of a garda that he permit a designated registered medical practitioner to take from him a specimen of his blood or, at his option, provide for the designated registered medical practitioner a specimen of his urine was quashed, there being no obligation to comply 'forthwith' in the particular subsection. On the other hand, in *State (Sugg) v. O'Sullivan*[56] it was held that the omission of the words 'a public place' from a conviction for dangerous driving did not invalidate the conviction where it recited that the offence had taken

---

53 Second edition, volume 1, p. 207.
54 *State (Cunningham) v. Ó Floinn* [1960] IR 198. It should be noted that a complaint, unlike a conviction, does not have to disclose that it is made in respect of a statutory offence: *Attorney General (McDonnell) v. Higgins* [1964] IR 374.
55 Unwritten judgment of the High Court (Egan J) delivered 19 February 1988.
56 Supra.

place at the junction of two roads. Certainty also requires that the conviction clearly show the precise offence in respect of which it is entered. So where a summons alleges more than one offence, the adjudication should deal with each offence and should not purport to convict the defendant generally of the offences charged. In *R. (Buck) v. Londonderry JJ*[57] a conviction for being under the influence of drink or drugs when 'driving or attempting to drive or when in charge of a motor car' was held bad.

8.16 Costs Under section 22(1) of the Road Traffic Act 1994 where a person is convicted of an offence under sections 49 or 50 of the 1961 Act or sections 13, 14 or 15 of the 1994 Act the court must, unless satisfied that there are special and substantial reasons for not doing so, order the person to pay a contribution towards the costs and expenses incurred by the Medical Bureau of Road Safety.[58] There is no reciprocal provision should a prosecution result in an acquittal. Rule 67 of the District Court Rules empowers a District Judge to award costs against any party in a case of summary jurisdiction other than the Attorney General or 'a member of the Garda Síochána acting in discharge of his duties as a police officer'.[59] But this rule does not apply in an appeal to the Circuit Court.[60]

---

57 [1952] NI 1.
58 The amount ordered to be paid is not to exceed the amount for the time being prescribed: currently £75 under the Road Traffic Act 1994 (Part III) Regulations, 1994, SI No. 351 of 1994.
59 The constitutionality of this exemption was upheld in *Dillane v. Ireland* [1980] ILRM 167.
60 *State (DPP) v. Roe* [1985] IR 307.

9

Appeals and other Review Procedures

APPEALS TO THE CIRCUIT COURT

9.01 The right to appeal and the procedure A defendant has a general right of appeal in criminal cases from the District Court.[1] An appeal may be brought even where a case has been dismissed under the Probation Act.[2] The appeal will lie to the Circuit Court judge within whose circuit the courthouse in which the order was made is situate.[3] Three documents are generally required under the District Court Rules to institute an appeal: a notice of appeal signed by the appellant or his solicitor must be lodged with the clerk of the court area in which the decision was given and a copy must be served on the opposing party within 14 days of the decision; a recognizance, with one or more sureties as directed by the District Judge, conditioned to prosecute the appeal may be entered into; and the appellant must sign a form of appeal specifying the place of sitting of the Circuit Court to which the appeal is taken.[4]

9.02 The effect of an appeal Where notice of appeal has been given and a recognizance has been entered into, the judge may not issue a warrant to execute the court order pending the hearing of the appeal or until the appellant has failed to perform the conditions of the recognizance.[5] If the appellant is in custody, he must be liberated on entering into the recognizance.[6] Where notice of appeal is lodged against a consequential or ancillary disqualification order, or against the conviction to which such an order is related, within 14 days of the making of the order and the appellant

---

1   Courts of Justice Act 1928 section 18(1).
2   Courts of Justice Act 1953 section 33.
3   Courts of Justice Act 1928 section 18(3) as amended by the Courts of Justice Act 1936 section 58.
4   For a detailed account of the procedure to be followed on instituting an appeal see Woods, *District Court Practice and Procedure in Criminal Cases* (Limerick, 1994), pp. 450-453.
5   DCR, 1948 r. 68 (7).
6   DCR, 1948 r. 194.

has entered into a recognizance to prosecute the appeal, the operation of the order stands suspended pending the appeal.[7]

9.03 The hearing of the appeal An appellant may appeal against conviction and sentence or against sentence only. An appeal against conviction and sentence entails a rehearing of the case against the defendant.[8] Any issue, whether of fact or law, may be reconsidered and either side may adduce new evidence.[9] However, a Circuit Court judge does not have jurisdiction to quash a District Court order on the ground of form, and it has been held that his refusal to embark on the merits of a case constituted a declining of jurisdiction in respect of which a mandamus should issue.[10] On hearing an appeal against conviction the Circuit Court may increase the sentence imposed in the District Court.[11] Where the appeal is against sentence only, the Circuit Court will not rehear the case except in so far as it is necessary to enable it to adjudicate on the question of sentence.[12] The Circuit Court may increase a sentence even though the appeal is confined to sentence.[13]

9.04 On the hearing of an appeal, the Circuit Court is empowered to 'confirm, vary or reverse' the order of the District Court.[14] But its jurisdiction is confined to the same limits as are imposed on the District Court.[15] Consequently, it cannot impose a penalty which could not have been imposed by the District Court. The Circuit Court may amend a summons, charge or information.[16] It also has jurisdiction to amend a conviction or order in the event of an omission or mistake in the making or drawing up of the conviction or order, or any variance between the facts stated in the conviction or order and the evidence adduced in support of it.[17] However, it is doubtful whether this power of amendment extends to

---

7   Section 30(3)(c) of the 1961 Act as substituted by section 20 of the 1968 Act.
8   *Attorney General (Lambe) v. Fitzgerald* [1973] IR 195.
9   *Ex parte McFadden* [1888] Judgments of the Superior Courts (Irl) 168; *Director of Public Prosecutions (Nagle) v. Flynn* [1987] IR 534; [1989] ILRM 65.
10 *State (Attorney General) v. Connolly* [1948] IR 176.
11 *State (Aherne) v. The Governor of Limerick Prison* [1982] IR 188; [1983] ILRM 17.
12 Courts (Supplemental Provisions) Act, 1961 section 50.
13 See the judgment of Walsh J in *State (Aherne) v. The Governor of Limerick Prison*, supra.
14 Petty Sessions (Ireland) Act 1851 section 24(6) and see *State (McLoughlin) v. Shannon* [1948] IR 439.
15 *State (White) v. Martin* (1977) 111 ILTR 21.
16 County Officers and Courts (Ireland) Act 1877 section 76.
17 Civil Bill Courts (Ireland) Act 1864 section 49.

points of substance.[18] The Circuit Court has the power to adjourn the hearing of an appeal, or to remit the matter to the District Judge who made the original order with such declarations or directions as seem proper.[19] On the determination of the appeal the judge may direct the county registrar to issue the warrant necessary to execute the original order or the order as varied.[20] If the order directs imprisonment, the judge may direct that the defendant be taken into custody forthwith, or detained in custody, and imprisoned pending the issue of the warrant.[21]

9.05 The decision of the Circuit Court on appeal is 'final and conclusive and not appealable'.[22] This does not, however, preclude an application to the High Court for judicial review.[23]

CASE STATED

9.06 **Appeal by case stated** A case stated allows for the opinion of the High Court to be sought on a question of law arising during the course of District Court proceedings. There are two distinct procedures. First, under section 2 of the Summary Jurisdiction Act 1857 as extended by section 51(1) of the Courts (Supplemental Provisions) Act 1961 any party to summary proceedings determined in the District Court, if dissatisfied with the determination as being erroneous on a point of law, may apply in writing within fourteen days to the judge to state and sign a case setting forth the facts and the grounds of the determination for the opinion of the High Court.[24] The judge may refuse to state a case where he is of the opinion that the application is frivolous; but he must not refuse an application made by or under the direction of the Director of Public Prosecutions.[25] In the event of a refusal an application may be made to the

---

18 R. v. Tomlinson (1872) LR 8 QB 12 and R. v. Padbury (1879) 5 QBD 126: cases where a power to amend under a comparable English statute was considered.
19 County Officers and Courts (Ireland) Act 1877 section 72.
20 CCR O. 43, r. 5.
21 CCR O. 43, r. 6 and see DCR, 1948 r. 198.
22 Courts of Justice Act 1928 section 18(3).
23 See, for example, State (Attorney General) v. Connolly [1948] IR 176 and State (McLoughlin) v. Shannon [1948] IR 439 and see State (McCarthy) v. O'Donnell [1945] IR 126 where the Supreme Court considered the effect of a statutory provision that a decision was to be 'final and conclusive'.
24 For the law and procedure relating to this form of case stated see Collins and O'Reilly, *Civil Proceedings and the State in Ireland: A Practitioner's Guide* (Dublin, 1990), chapter 1 and Woods, op. cit., pp. 466-477.
25 Summary Jurisdiction Act 1857 section 4 and the Prosecution of Offences Act 1974 section 3(1) and DCR, 1948 r. 202.

High Court for an order calling on the judge to show cause why the case should not be stated.[26] Where the judge grants an application for a case stated, the determination in respect of which the application is made will be suspended until the case stated has been heard and determined.[27] Where the application is refused, the determination will be suspended until the judge refuses.[28] On hearing the case stated the High Court is empowered to reverse, affirm or amend the determination; or to remit the matter to the judge with its opinion thereon; or to make such other order in relation to the matter as may seem fit.[29] The order of the High Court is final and conclusive subject to a right of appeal to the Supreme Court.[30] A person who utilises the procedure will be taken to have abandoned his right of appeal.[31] But where the case stated does not give rise to a complete and final determination, an appeal may still lie from the decision of the District Court.[32]

9.07 Consultative case stated The second case stated procedure is provided for in section 52 of the Courts (Supplemental Provisions) Act 1961 which provides that a District Judge may refer a question of law arising in summary proceedings to the High Court for determination; and he must refer any such question, where he is asked to do so by a person who has been heard in the proceedings, unless he considers the request is frivolous.[33] But the District Judge has no right to ask the High Court to answer questions extraneous to the issues before him; the only question of law he may refer is one which actually arises.[34]

9.08 Some practical differences A number of practical differences may be noted between the two case stated procedures. The District Judge may take the initiative and state a case under the 1961 Act without being

---

26 Summary Jurisdiction Act 1857 section 5 and see *State (Turley) v. Ó Floinn* [1968] IR 245; *Sports Arena Ltd v. O'Reilly* [1987] IR 185.
27 Courts (Supplemental Provisions) Act 1961 section 51(2).
28 Ibid.
29 Summary Jurisdiction Act 1857 section 6 as amended by the Courts (Supplemental Provisions) Act 1961 section 51(3).
30 Ibid. and see *Attorney General (Fahy) v. Bruen* [1936] IR 750; (1936) 70 ILTR 247.
31 Summary Jurisdiction Act 1857 section 14 as amended by the Courts (Supplemental Provisions) Act 1961 section 51(3).
32 *R. (Drohan) v. Waterford JJ* [1900] 2 IR 307.
33 As to procedure see Collins and O'Reilly, op. cit., chapter 2, paras. 2.2-2.13 and Woods, op. cit., pp. 477-481.
34 *Attorney General v. McLoughlin* [1931] IR 430.

asked to do so. And a case may be stated under the 1961 Act before the judge has made his determination, whereas a case stated under the 1857 Act follows on his determination. There is no statutory mechanism for reviewing a judge's refusal to state a case under the 1961 Act, whereas such a mechanism is provided under the 1857 Act.[35] No statutory provision is made as to the effect of a case stated under the 1961 Act, pending its outcome, on any decision made by the judge. Nor is provision made whereby a case stated under the 1961 Act prejudices the defendant's right of appeal. Lastly, an appeal to the Supreme Court from a decision of the High Court given pursuant to a case stated under the 1961 Act requires the leave of the High Court;[36] no leave is required where the case has been stated under the 1857 Act.

JUDICIAL REVIEW

9.09 Since 1986 the old state side procedure has been replaced by a judicial review procedure, now contained in order 84 of the Rules of the Superior Courts, so that the remedies, certiorari, mandamus, prohibition and quo warranto, may now be sought as part of an application for judicial review.[37] Of these orders certiorari is sometimes sought in drunken driving cases: it is an order of the High Court directed to an inferior tribunal requiring it to deliver up its order so that it may be quashed.

9.10 When an order may be granted The circumstances in which an order of certiorari may be granted were formulated by Gibson J in *R. (Martin) v. Mahony*:[38] '(a) where there is want or excess of jurisdiction when the enquiry begins or during its progress; (b) when in the exercise of jurisdiction there is error on the face of the adjudication; (c) where there has been an abuse of jurisdiction . . . or disregard of the essentials of justice . . .; (d) where the Court is shown to be disqualified by likelihood of bias or by interest; (e) where there is fraud.' Certiorari does not lie where it is alleged that the decision of the inferior tribunal was based on inadequate evidence. Thus in *Lennon v. Clifford*[39] O'Hanlon J approved the following statement of principle taken from *Halsbury's Laws of England*:[40]

---

35 See *State (Turley) v Ó Floinn* [1968] IR 245.
36 Courts (Supplemental Provisions) Act 1961 section 52(2); *Minister for Justice v Wang Zhu Jie* [1993] 1 IR 426; [1991] ILRM 823.
37 See Collins and O'Reilly, op. cit., chapter 4 and Woods, op. cit., pp. 487-502.
38 [1910] 2 IR 695, 731.
39 [1992] 1 IR 382; [1993] ILRM 77.
40 3rd edition, vol. 11, para. 119.

> Where the proceedings are regular on their face and the inferior tribunal had jurisdiction, the superior court will not grant the order of certiorari on the ground that the inferior tribunal had misconceived a point of law. When the inferior tribunal has jurisdiction to decide a matter, it cannot (merely because it . . . misconstrues a statute, or admits illegal evidence, or rejects legal evidence, or misdirects itself as to the weight of the evidence, or convicts without evidence) be deemed to exceed or abuse its jurisdiction. . . . Certiorari will not be granted to quash the decision of an inferior tribunal within its jurisdiction on the ground that the decision is wrong in matters of fact, and the Court will not hear evidence impeaching the decision on the facts. . . . If there is any evidence, the Court will not examine whether the right conclusion has been drawn from it.

In the same judgment[41] O'Hanlon J observed that: 'The general tenor of the decisions is that the High Court is not available as a court of appeal from decisions of other tribunals except where it is given such a function by statute, and that the scope for challenging the validity of orders made by lower courts by way of judicial review proceedings is confined to those cases where reliance can be placed on want of jurisdiction, or excess of jurisdiction; some clear departure from fair and constitutional procedures; bias by interest; fraud and perjury; or decisions containing an error of law apparent on the face of the record.' The grounds on which an order of certiorari may be granted which have particular relevance to drunken driving prosecutions are: want or excess of jurisdiction, error on the face of the record and failure to observe the requirements of constitutional or natural justice.

9.11 Want or excess of jurisdiction A District Judge would, for example, be acting without jurisdiction where he imposes a penalty in excess of that laid down by the statute. In such a case both conviction and penalty could be quashed by certiorari as the court will not sever the conviction.[42] Likewise where a judge deals with a matter which is outside the territorial limits of his jurisdiction he acts without jurisdiction.[43] In recent years the scope of the concept of jurisdiction has widened, as

---

41 At p. 386 of the report.
42 See the judgment of O'Daly J (as he then was) in *State (Caddle) v. McCarthy* [1957] IR 359 and the decisions of the Supreme Court in *State (Kiernan) v. de Burca* [1963] IR 348; (1965) 99 ILTR 14 and in *State (de Burca) v. Ó hUadhaigh* [1976] IR 85.
43 *State (Reilly) v The Circuit Court Judge of the Midland Circuit* [1936] IR 372; (1936) 70 ILTR 105.

evidenced by the observations of Gannon J in *State (Healy) v. Donoghue*:[44]

> Before dealing with the submissions on the grounds on which the conditional orders were made, I think I should say at the outset that it appears to me that the determination of the question of whether or not a court of local and limited jurisdiction is acting within its jurisdiction is not confined to an examination of the statutory limits of jurisdiction imposed on the court. It appears to me that this question involves also an examination of whether or not the court is performing the basic function for which it is established—the administration of justice. Even if all the formalities of the statutory limitation of the court be complied with and if the court procedures are formally satisfied, it is my opinion that the court in such instance is not acting within its jurisdiction if, at the same time, the person accused is deprived of any of his basic rights of justice at a criminal trial.

In England Lord Denning[45] has gone so far as to suggest that where an inferior tribunal makes an error of law, on which the decision in the case depends, then it acts without jurisdiction. But it does not appear that the Irish courts would agree with this proposition.[46]

9.12 Error on the face of the record According to O'Connor's *Justice of the Peace*,[47] certiorari may be applied for where 'the order is bad upon its face for uncertainty, duplicity, failing to contain all necessary averments to constitute the offence, failing to show jurisdiction or otherwise. . . .' Thus in *State (Cunningham) v. Ó Floinn*[48] certiorari was granted to quash convictions which did not disclose that the offences were statutory.

9.13 Failure to comply with the requirements of constitutional or natural justice Certiorari will lie where a conviction has been obtained in disregard of the essentials of justice. Consequently, convictions obtained where the defendant has not been summoned and does not appear, or where the defendant has not been allowed to call witnesses, are liable to

---

44 [1976] IR 325, 333.
45 In *Pearlman v. Harrow School* [1979] QB 56, 70.
46 See *State (Davidson) v. Farrell* [1960] IR 438; *Lennon v. Clifford* [1992] 1 IR 382 [1993] ILRM 77.
47 Second edition, volume 1, p. 329.
48 [1960] IR 198. See also *Butler v. Mahon*, unwritten judgment of the High Court (Egan J) delivered 19 February 1988, para. 8.15 ante.

be quashed.[49] It has often been said that the courts must in their procedures observe the rules of natural justice: 'nemo iudex in causa sua' and 'audi alteram partem'. In other words, an accused is entitled to trial by an impartial tribunal and to be heard in his own defence. The more recent cases tend to express these requirements in terms of 'constitutional justice' or 'fair procedures'. Thus in *State (Healy) v. Donoghue*[50] O'Higgins CJ held that article 38 of the Constitution makes it 'mandatory that every criminal trial shall be conducted in accordance with the concept of justice, that the procedures applied shall be fair, and that the person accused will be afforded every opportunity to defend himself'.

9.14 The procedure The procedure on a certiorari application is governed by order 84 of the Rules of the Superior Courts. An application must first be made for leave to apply for judicial review; this application is made by ex parte motion grounded on a statement of grounds in the prescribed form and an affidavit verifying the facts relied on.[51] If leave is granted, the application for judicial review is then made by originating notice of motion unless the court directs that it be made by plenary summons.[52] An applicant seeking an order of certiorari must lodge in the High Court a copy of any order or conviction which he seeks to have quashed or account for his failure to do so.[53] A respondent who intends to oppose the application must file in the Central Office a statement setting out his grounds of opposition and an affidavit verifying any facts relied on in the statement, and serve a copy of the statement and affidavit on all parties.[54] In addition, the court may, on the hearing of the application, hear any person who appears to be a proper person to be heard notwithstanding that he has not been served with the applicant's notice of motion or summons.[55] Where an order of certiorari is made it will direct that the proceedings impugned be quashed forthwith on their removal into the High Court.[56] But as well as quashing a decision, the High Court may remit it to the inferior tribunal with a direction to reconsider it and reach a decision in accordance with the findings of the court.[57]

---

49 See the judgment of Gibson J in *R. (Martin) v. Mahony* [1910] 2 IR 695. The requirements in relation to the conduct of a trial are discussed at paras. 8.02-8.03 ante.
50 [1976] IR 325, 349.
51 RSC O. 84, r. 20. See *G. v. Director of Public Prosecutions* [1994] 1 IR 374.
52 RSC O. 84, r. 22(1).
53 RSC O. 84, r. 26(2).
54 RSC O. 84, r. 22(4).
55 RSC O. 84, r. 26(1).
56 RSC O. 84, r. 26(3).
57 RSC O. 84, r. 26(4), as for example happened in *Singh v. Ruane* [1989] IR 610 and *Coughlan v. Patwell* [1993] 1

9.15 Certiorari and an appeal There is clear authority that certiorari will not be granted where an appeal is pending in the same matter.[58] Nevertheless, the Rules of the Superior Courts expressly contemplate the adjournment of an application for leave to apply for an order of certiorari 'until the appeal is determined or the time for appealing has expired'.[59] The better view would now appear to be that the existence of an appeal will not of itself preclude the High Court from intervening in an appropriate case. In *Duff v. Mangan*[60] Denham J quoted with approval the following words of O'Higgins CJ in *State (Abenglen Properties Ltd) v. Dublin Corporation*:[61]

> The question . . . arises as to the effect of the existence of a right of appeal or an alternative remedy on the exercise of the court's discretion. It is well established that the existence of such right or remedy ought not to prevent the court from acting. It seems to me to be a question of justice. The court ought to take into account all the circumstances of the case, including the purpose for which certiorari has been sought, the adequacy of the alternative remedy and, of course, the conduct of the applicant. If the decision impugned is made without jurisdiction or in breach of natural justice then, normally, the existence of a right of appeal or of a failure to avail of such, should be immaterial. Again, if an appeal can only deal with the merits and not with the question of jurisdiction involved, the existence of such ought not to be a ground for refusing relief. Other than these, there may be cases where the decision exhibits an error of law and a perfectly simple appeal can rectify the complaint. . . . In such cases, while retaining always the power to quash, a court should be slow to do so unless satisfied that, for some particular reason, the appeal or alternative remedy is not adequate.

REMISSION

9.16 Under section 23 of the Criminal Justice Act 1951 the Government may remit a punishment or disqualification imposed by a court exercising

---

IR 31, but not in *Dawson v. Hamill* [1991] 1 IR 213 in *Sweeney v. Brophy* [1993] 2 IR 202 nor in *Dineen v. Delap* [1994] 2 IR 228. See Costello, 'Certiorari followed by remittal' (1993) 3 ICLJ 145.

58 *State (Roche) v. Delap* [1980] IR 170; *Devereaux v. Kotsonouris* [1992] ILRM 140.
59 RSC O. 84, r. 20(5).
60 [1994] 1 ILRM 91.
61 [1984] IR 381, 393; [1982] ILRM 590.

criminal jurisdiction and may delegate this power to the Minister for Justice. However, section 124 of the Road Traffic Act 1961 forbids the remission of a disqualification from holding a driving licence imposed under the Act.

Appendix A

Road Traffic Act 1994

PART III

Driving Offences

9.—(1) In this Part— <small>Interpretation of Part III</small>
'analysis' includes any operation used in determining the concentration of alcohol in a specimen of breath, blood or urine, and any operation used in determining the presence (if any) of a drug or drugs in a specimen of blood or urine, and cognate words shall be construed accordingly;
'Bureau' has the meaning assigned to it by section 37(1) of the Act of 1968;
'designated' means designated by a member of the Garda Síochána;
'doctor' means a person registered in the General Register of Medical Practitioners established under section 26 of the Medical Practitioners Act 1978;
'intoxicant' includes alcohol and drugs and any combination of drugs or of drugs and alcohol.

(2) A reference in this Part (other than sections 10 and 11) to section 49 or 50 of the Principal Act is to the section inserted by this Part.

10.—The following section is inserted in the Principal Act in substitution for section 49 of that Act: <small>Prohibition on driving vehicle while under influence of intoxicant</small>

'49.—(1)(a) A person shall not drive or attempt to drive a mechanically propelled vehicle in a public place while he is under the influence of an intoxicant to such an extent as to be incapable of having proper control of the vehicle.

(b) In this subsection 'intoxicant' includes alcohol and drugs and any combination of drugs or of drugs and alcohol.

(2) A person shall not drive or attempt to drive a mechanically propelled vehicle in a public place while there is present in his body a quantity of alcohol such that, within 3 hours after so driving or attempting to drive, the concentration of alcohol in his blood will exceed a concentration of 80 milligrammes of alcohol per 100 millilitres of blood.

(3) A person shall not drive or attempt to drive a mechanically propelled vehicle in a public place while there is present in his body a quantity of alcohol such that,

within 3 hours after so driving or attempting to drive, the concentration of alcohol in his urine will exceed a concentration of 107 milligrammes of alcohol per 100 millilitres of urine.

(4) A person shall not drive or attempt to drive a mechanically propelled vehicle in a public place while there is present in his body a quantity of alcohol such that, within 3 hours after so driving or attempting to drive, the concentration of alcohol in his breath will exceed a concentration of 35 microgrammes of alcohol per 100 millilitres of breath.

(5)(*a*) The Minister may, by regulations made by him, vary the concentration of alcohol for the time being standing specified in subsection (2), (3) or (4) of this section, whether generally or in respect of a particular class of person, and the said subsection shall have effect in accordance with any such regulations for the time being in force.

(*b*) A draft of every regulation proposed to be made under this subsection shall be laid before each House of the Oireachtas and the regulation shall not be made until a resolution approving of the draft has been passed by each such House and section 5(2) of this Act shall not apply to a regulation made under this subsection.

(6)(*a*) A person who contravenes subsection (1), (2), (3) or (4) of this section shall be guilty of an offence and shall be liable on summary conviction to a fine not exceeding £1,000 or to imprisonment for a term not exceeding 6 months or to both.

(*b*) A person charged with an offence under this section may, in lieu of being found guilty of that offence, be found guilty of an offence under section 50 of this Act.

(7) Section 1(1) of the Probation of Offenders Act 1907 shall not apply to an offence under this section.

(8) A member of the Garda Síochána may arrest without warrant a person who in the member's opinion is committing or has committed an offence under this section.'

Prohibition on being in charge of vehicle while under influence of intoxicant

11.—The following section is inserted in the Principal Act in substitution for section 50 of that Act:

'50.—(1)(*a*) A person shall be guilty of an offence if, when in charge of a mechanically propelled vehicle in a public place with intent to drive or attempt to drive the vehicle (but not driving or attempting to drive it), he is under the influence of an intoxicant to such an extent as to be incapable of having proper control of the vehicle.

(*b*) In this subsection 'intoxicant' includes alcohol and drugs and any combination of drugs or of drugs and alcohol.

(2) A person shall be guilty of an offence if, when in charge of a mechanically propelled vehicle in a public place with intent to drive or attempt to drive the vehicle (but not driving or attempting to drive it), there is present in his body a quantity of alcohol such that, within 3 hours after so being in charge, the concentration of alcohol in his blood will exceed a concentration of 80 milligrammes of alcohol per 100 millilitres of blood.

(3) A person shall be guilty of an offence if, when in charge of a mechanically

Appendix A

propelled vehicle in a public place with intent to drive or attempt to drive the vehicle (but not driving or attempting to drive it), there is present in his body a quantity of alcohol such that, within 3 hours after so being in charge, the concentration of alcohol in his urine will exceed a concentration of 107 milligrammes of alcohol per 100 millilitres of urine.

(4) A person shall be guilty of an offence if, when in charge of a mechanically propelled vehicle in a public place with intent to drive or attempt to drive the vehicle (but not driving or attempting to drive it), there is present in his body a quantity of alcohol such that, within 3 hours after so being in charge, the concentration of alcohol in his breath will exceed a concentration of 35 microgrammes of alcohol per 100 millilitres of breath.

(5)(a) The Minister may, by regulations made by him, vary the concentration of alcohol for the time being standing specified in subsection (2), (3) or (4) of this section, whether generally or in respect of a particular class of person, and the said subsection shall have effect in accordance with any such regulations for the time being in force.

(b) A draft of every regulation proposed to be made under this subsection shall be laid before each House of the Oireachtas and the regulation shall not be made until a resolution approving of the draft has been passed by each such House and section 5(2) of this Act shall not apply to a regulation made under this subsection.

(6)(a) A person guilty of an offence under this section shall be liable on summary conviction to a fine not exceeding £1,000 or to imprisonment for a term not exceeding 6 months or to both.

(b) A person charged with an offence under this section may, in lieu of being found guilty of that offence, be found guilty of an offence under section 49 of this Act.

(7) Section 1(1) of the Probation of Offenders Act 1907 shall not apply to an offence under this section.

(8) In a prosecution for an offence under this section it shall be presumed that the defendant intended to drive or attempt to drive the vehicle concerned until he shows the contrary.

(9) A person liable to be charged with an offence under this section shall not, by reference to the same occurrence, be liable to be charged under section 12 of the Licensing Act 1872, with the offence of being drunk while in charge, on a highway or other public place, of a carriage.

(10) A member of the Garda Síochána may arrest without warrant a person who in the member's opinion is committing or has committed an offence under this section.'

12.—(1) Whenever a member of the Garda Síochána is of opinion that a person in charge of a mechanically propelled vehicle in a public place has consumed intoxicating liquor, he may require the person— [Obligation to provide preliminary breath specimen]

(a) to provide, by exhaling into an apparatus for indicating the presence of alcohol in the breath, a specimen of his breath and may indicate the manner in which he is to comply with the requirement;

(b) to accompany him to a place (including a vehicle) at or in the vicinity of that public place and there require him to provide, by exhaling into such an apparatus, a specimen of his breath and may indicate the manner in which he is to comply with the requirement;

(c) where he does not have such an apparatus with him, to remain at that place in his presence or in the presence of another member of the Garda Síochána until such an apparatus becomes available to him (but he shall not require him to so remain for more than one hour) and he may then require the person to provide, by exhaling into such an apparatus, a specimen of his breath and may indicate the manner in which he is to comply with the requirement.

(2) A person who refuses or fails to comply forthwith with a requirement under this section, or to comply forthwith with such a requirement in a manner indicated by a member of the Garda Síochána, shall be guilty of an offence and shall be liable on summary conviction to a fine not exceeding £1,000 or to imprisonment for a term not exceeding 6 months or to both.

(3) A member of the Garda Síochána may arrest without warrant a person who in the member's opinion is committing or has committed an offence under this section.

(4) In a prosecution for an offence under this Part or under section 49 or 50 of the Principal Act it shall be presumed, until the contrary is shown, that an apparatus provided by a member of the Garda Síochána for the purpose of enabling a person to provide a specimen of breath pursuant to this section is an apparatus for indicating the presence of alcohol in the breath.

Obligation to provide specimen following arrest

13.—(1) Where a person is arrested under section 49(8) or 50(10) of the Principal Act or section 12(3), or where a person is arrested under section 53(6), 106(3A) or 112(6) of the Principal Act and a member of the Garda Síochána is of opinion that the person has consumed an intoxicant, a member of the Garda Síochána may, at a Garda Síochána station, at his discretion, do either or both of the following–

(a) require the person to provide, by exhaling into an apparatus for determining the concentration of alcohol in the breath, 2 specimens of his breath and may indicate the manner in which he is to comply with the requirement,

(b) require the person either—

(i) to permit a designated doctor to take from the person a specimen of his blood, or

(ii) at the option of the person, to provide for the designated doctor a specimen of his urine,

and if the doctor states in writing that he is unwilling, on medical grounds, to take from the person or be provided by him with the specimen to which the requirement in either of the foregoing subparagraphs related, the member may make a requirement of the person under this paragraph in relation to the specimen other than that to which the first requirement related.

(2) Subject to section 23, a person who refuses or fails to comply forthwith with a requirement under subsection (1)(a) shall be guilty of an offence and shall

be liable on summary conviction to a fine not exceeding £1,000 or to imprisonment for a term not exceeding 6 months or to both.

(3) Subject to section 23, a person who, following a requirement under subsection (1)(*b*)—
   (*a*) refuses or fails to comply with the requirement, or
   (*b*) refuses or fails to comply with a requirement of a designated doctor in relation to the taking under that subsection of a specimen of blood or the provision under that subsection of a specimen of urine,

shall be guilty of an offence and shall be liable on summary conviction to a fine not exceeding £1,000 or to imprisonment for a term not exceeding 6 months or to both.

(4) In a prosecution for an offence under this Part or under section 49 or 50 of the Principal Act it shall be presumed, until the contrary is shown, that an apparatus provided by a member of the Garda Síochána for the purpose of enabling a person to provide 2 specimens of breath pursuant to this section is an apparatus for determining the concentration of alcohol in the breath.

(5) Section 1(1) of the Probation of Offenders Act 1907 shall not apply to an offence under this section.

14.—(1) Whenever a member of the Garda Síochána is of opinion that a person in charge of a mechanically propelled vehicle in a public place is under the influence of a drug or drugs to such an extent as to be incapable of having proper control of the vehicle, he may require the person to accompany him to a Garda Síochána station. *Obligation to accompany member to Garda Síochána station, not under arrest, to provide blood or urine specimen*

(2) A person who refuses or fails to comply with a requirement under subsection (1) shall be guilty of an offence and shall be liable on summary conviction to a fine not exceeding £1,000 or to imprisonment for a term not exceeding 6 months or to both.

(3) A member of the Garda Síochána may arrest without warrant a person who in the member's opinion is committing or has committed an offence under subsection (2).

(4) Where a person is at a Garda Síochána station either pursuant to subsection (1) or having been arrested under subsection (3), a member of the Garda Síochána may there require the person either—
   (*a*) to permit a designated doctor to take from the person a specimen of his blood, or
   (*b*) at the option of the person, to provide for the designated doctor a specimen of his urine,

and if the doctor states in writing that he is unwilling, on medical grounds, to take from the person or be provided by him with the specimen to which the requirement in either of the foregoing paragraphs related, the member may make a requirement of the person under this subsection in relation to the specimen other than that to which the first requirement related.

(5) Subject to section 23, a person who, following a requirement under subsection (4)—
   (*a*) refuses or fails to comply with the requirement, or
   (*b*) refuses or fails to comply with a requirement of a designated doctor in

relation to the taking under that subsection of a specimen of blood or the provision under that subsection of a specimen of urine,

shall be guilty of an offence and shall be liable on summary conviction to a fine not exceeding £1,000 or to imprisonment for a term not exceeding 6 months or to both.

(6) Section 1(1) of the Probation of Offenders Act 1907 shall not apply to an offence under this section.

<small>Obligation to provide blood or urine specimen while in hospital</small>

15.—(1) Where, in a public place, an event occurs in relation to a mechanically propelled vehicle in consequence of which a person is injured, or claims or appears to have been injured, and is admitted to, or attends at, a hospital and a member of the Garda Síochána is of opinion that, at the time of the event,—

(*a*) the person was driving or attempting to drive, or in charge of with intent to drive or attempt to drive (but not driving or attempting to drive), the mechanically propelled vehicle, and

(*b*) the person had consumed an intoxicant,

then such member may, in the hospital, require the person either—

(i) to permit a designated doctor to take from the person a specimen of his blood, or

(ii) at the option of the person, to provide for the designated doctor a specimen of his urine,

and if the doctor states in writing that he is unwilling, on medical grounds, to take from the person or be provided by him with the specimen to which the requirement in either of the foregoing subparagraphs related, the member may make a requirement of the person under this subsection in relation to the specimen other than that to which the first requirement related.

(2) Subject to section 23, a person who, following a requirement under subsection (1)—

(*a*) refuses or fails to comply with the requirement, or

(*b*) refuses or fails to comply with a requirement of a designated doctor in relation to the taking under that subsection of a specimen of blood or the provision under that subsection of a specimen of urine,

shall be guilty of an offence and shall be liable on summary conviction to a fine not exceeding £1,000 or to imprisonment for a term not exceeding 6 months or to both.

(3) Notwithstanding subsection (2), it shall not be an offence for a person to refuse or fail to comply with a requirement under subsection (1) where, following his admission to, or attendance at, a hospital, the person comes under the care of a doctor and the doctor refuses, on medical grounds, to permit the taking or provision of the specimen concerned.

(4) Section 1(1) of the Probation of offenders Act 1907 shall not apply to an offence under this section.

<small>Detention of intoxicated drivers where a danger to selves or others</small>

16.—(1) Where a person is—

(*a*) at a Garda Síochána station having been arrested under section 49(8) or 50(10) of the Principal Act or section 12(3) or 14(3), or

(*b*) required under section 14(1) to accompany a member of the Garda

Síochána to a Garda Síochána station and complies with the requirement,
he may, at the Garda Síochána station, if the member of the Garda Síochána for the time being in charge of the station is of opinion that the person is under the influence of an intoxicant to such an extent as to be a threat to the safety of himself or others, be detained in custody for such period (not exceeding 6 hours from the time of his arrest or, as the case may be, from the time he was required to accompany a member to the station) as the member of the Garda Síochána so in charge considers necessary.

(2) Where a person is detained under subsection (1), the member of the Garda Síochána for the time being in charge of the Garda Síochána station shall—
- (a) in case the person detained is or the said member is of opinion that he is 18 years of age or more, as soon as is practicable, if it is reasonably possible to do so, inform a relative of the person or such other person as the person so detained may specify of the detention, unless the person so detained does not wish any person to be so informed, and
- (b) in case the person detained is or the said member is of opinion that he is under the age of 18 years, as soon as is practicable, if it is reasonably possible to do so, inform a relative of the person or such other person as the person so detained may specify of the detention.

(3) A person detained under subsection (1) shall—
- (a) in case he is or the member of the Garda Síochána for the time being in charge of the Garda Síochána station is of opinion that he is 18 years of age or more, upon the attendance at the station of a person being either a relative of, or a person specified pursuant to subsection (2) by, the person so detained, be released by the said member into the custody of that person, unless—
  - (i) the latter person is or the said member is of opinion that he is under the age of 18 years,
  - (ii) the person so detained does not wish to be released into the custody of the latter person, or
  - (iii) the member aforesaid is of opinion that the person so detained continues to be under the influence of an intoxicant to such an extent that, if he is then released into the custody of the latter person, he will continue to be a threat to the safety of himself or others,

  and shall, if not so released, be released at the expiration of the period of detention authorised by subsection (1), and
- (b) in case he is or the member of the Garda Síochána for the time being in charge of the Garda Síochána station is of opinion that he is under the age of 18 years, upon the attendance at the station of a person being either a relative of, or a person specified pursuant to subsection (2) by, the person so detained, be released by the said member into the custody of that person, unless the latter person is or the said member is of opinion that he is under the age of 18 years, and shall, if not so released, be released at the expiration of the period of detention authorised by subsection (1).

Procedure following provision of breach specimen under section 13

17.—(1) Where, consequent on a requirement under section 13(1)(a) of him, a person provides 2 specimens of his breath and the apparatus referred to in that section determines the concentration of alcohol in each specimen—

    (a) in case the apparatus determines that each specimen has the same concentration of alcohol, either specimen, and

    (b) in case the apparatus determines that each specimen has a different concentration of alcohol, the specimen with the lower concentration of alcohol,

shall be taken into account for the purposes of sections 49(4) and 45(4) of the Principal Act and the other specimen shall be disregarded.

(2) Where the apparatus referred to in section 13(1) determines that in respect of the specimen of breath to be taken into account as aforesaid the person may have contravened section 49(4) or 50(4) of the Principal Act, he shall be supplied forthwith by a member of the Garda Síochána with 2 identical statements, automatically produced by the said apparatus in the prescribed form and duly completed by the member in the prescribed manner, stating the concentration of alcohol in the said specimen determined by the said apparatus.

(3) On receipt of the statements aforesaid, the person shall on being requested so to do by the member aforesaid—

    (a) forthwith acknowledge such receipt by placing his signature on each statement, and

    (b) thereupon return either of the statements to the member.

(4) A person who refuses or fails to comply with subsection (3) shall be guilty of an offence and shall be liable on summary conviction to a fine not exceeding £500 or to imprisonment for a term not exceeding 3 months or to both.

(5) Section 21(1) shall apply to a statement under this section as respects which there has been a failure to comply with subsection (3)(a) as it applies to a duly completed statement under this section.

Procedure regarding taking of specimens of blood and provisions of specimens of urine

18.—(1) Where under this Part a designated doctor has taken a specimen of blood from a person or has been provided by the person with a specimen of his urine, the doctor shall divide the specimen into 2 parts, place each part in a container which he shall forthwith seal and complete the form prescribed for the purposes of this section.

(2) Where a specimen of blood or urine of a person has been divided into 2 parts pursuant to subsection (1), a member of the Garda Síochána shall offer to the person one of the sealed containers together with a statement in writing indicating that he may retain either of the containers.

(3) As soon as practicable after subsection (2) has been complied with, a member of the Garda Síochána shall cause to be forwarded to the Bureau the completed form referred to in subsection (1), together with the relevant sealed container or, where the person has declined to retain one of the sealed containers, both relevant sealed containers.

(4) In a prosecution for an offence under this Part or under section 49 or 50 of the Principal Act, it shall be presumed until the contrary is shown that subsections (1) to (3) have been complied with.

Appendix A

19.—(1) As soon as practicable after it has received a specimen forwarded to it under section 18, the Bureau shall analyse the specimen and determine the concentration of alcohol or (as may be appropriate) the presence of a drug or drugs in the specimen.

(2) Where the Bureau receives 2 specimens of blood so forwarded together in relation to the same person or 2 specimens of urine so forwarded together in relation to the same person, it shall be sufficient compliance with subsection (1) for the Bureau to make an analysis of and determination in relation to one of the 2 specimens of blood or (as may be appropriate) one of the 2 specimens of urine.

(3) As soon as practicable after compliance with subsection (1), the Bureau shall forward to the Garda Síochána station from which the specimen analysed was forwarded a completed certificate in the form prescribed for the purpose of this section and shall forward a copy of the completed certificate to the person who is named on the relevant form under section 18 as the person from whom the specimen was taken or who provided it.

(4) In a prosecution for an offence under this Part or under section 49 or 50 of the Principal Act, it shall be presumed until the contrary is shown that subsections (1) to (3) have been complied with.

20.—(1) On the hearing of a charge for an offence under section 49 or 50 of the Principal Act, it shall not be necessary to show that the defendant had not consumed intoxicating liquor after the time when the offence is alleged to have been committed but before the taking or provision of a specimen under section 13, 14 or 15.

(2) Where, on the hearing of a charge for an offence under section 49 or 50 of the Principal Act, evidence is given by or on behalf of the defendant that, after the time when the offence is alleged to have been committed but before the taking or provision of a specimen under section 13, 14 or 15, he had consumed intoxicating liquor, the court shall disregard the evidence unless satisfied by or on behalf of the defendant—
- (a) that, but for that consumption, the concentration of alcohol in the defendant's blood (as specified in a certificate under section 19) would not have exceeded the concentration of alcohol for the time being standing specified in subsection (2) of the said section 49 or 50, as may be appropriate, whether generally or in respect of the class of person of which the defendant is a member,
- (b) that, but for that consumption, the concentration of alcohol in the defendant's urine (as specified in a certificate under section 19) would not have exceeded the concentration of alcohol for the time being standing specified in subsection 30(3) of the said section 49 or 50, as may be appropriate, whether generally or in respect of the class of person of which the defendant is a member, or
- (c) that, but for that consumption, the concentration of alcohol in the defendant's breath (as specified in a statement under section 17) would not have exceeded the concentration of alcohol for the time being standing specified in subsection (4) of the said section 49 or 50, as may be appropriate, whether generally or in respect of the class of

person of which the defendant is a member.

(3)(a) A person shall not take or attempt to take any action (including consumption of alcohol but excluding a refusal or failure to provide a specimen of his breath or urine or to permit the taking of a specimen of his blood) with the intention of frustrating a prosecution under section 49 or 50 of the Principal Act.

(b) A person who contravenes this subsection shall be guilty of an offence and shall be liable on summary conviction to a fine not exceeding £1,000 or to imprisonment for a term not exceeding 6 months or to both.

(4) Where, on the hearing of a charge for an offence under section 49 or 50 of the Principal Act, the court is satisfied that any action taken by the defendant (including consumption of alcohol but excluding a refusal or failure to provide a specimen of his breath or urine or to permit the taking of a specimen of his blood) was so taken with the intention of frustrating a prosecution under either of those sections, the court may find him guilty of an offence under subsection (3).

Provisions regarding certain evidence in proceedings under Road Traffic Acts 1961 to 1994

21.—(1) A duly completed statement purporting to have been supplied under section 17 shall, until the contrary is shown be sufficient evidence in any proceedings under the Road Traffic Acts 1961 to 1994 of the facts stated therein, without proof of any signature on it or that the signatory was the proper person to sign it, and shall, until the contrary is shown, be sufficient evidence of compliance by the member of the Garda Síochána concerned with the requirements imposed on him by or under this Part prior to and in connection with the supply by him pursuant to section 17(2) of such statement.

(2) A duly completed form under section 18 shall, until the contrary is shown, be sufficient evidence in any proceedings under the Road Traffic Acts 1961 to 1994 of the facts stated therein, without proof of any signature on it or that the signatory was the proper person to sign it, and shall, until the contrary is shown, be sufficient evidence of compliance by the designated doctor concerned with the requirements imposed on him by or under this Part.

(3) A certificate expressed to have been issued under section 19 shall, until the contrary is shown, be sufficient evidence in any proceedings under the Road Traffic Acts 1961 to 1994 of the facts stated therein, without proof of any signature on it or that the signatory was the proper person to sign it, and shall, until the contrary is shown, be sufficient evidence of compliance by the Bureau with the requirements imposed on it by or under this Part or Part V of the Act of 1968.

(4) In a prosecution for an offence under section 49 or 50 of the Principal Act or section 13, 14 or 15 it shall be presumed until the contrary is shown that each of the following persons is a designated doctor—

(a) a person who by virtue of powers conferred on him by this Part took from another person a specimen of that other person's blood or was provided by another person with a specimen of that other person's urine,

(b) a person for whom, following a requirement under section 13(1), 14(4) or 15(1) to permit the taking by him of a specimen of blood, there was a refusal or failure to give such permission or to comply with a

Appendix A 131

   requirement of his in relation to the taking of such a specimen,
  (c) a person for whom, following a requirement under section 13(1), 14(4) or 15(1) to provide for him a specimen of urine, there was a refusal or failure to provide such a specimen or to comply with a requirement of his in relation to the provision of such a specimen.

 (5) Where, pursuant to section 13, 14 or 15, a designated doctor states in writing that he is unwilling, on medical grounds, to take from a person a specimen of his blood or be provided by him with a specimen of his urine, the statement signed by the doctor shall, in any proceedings under the Road Traffic Acts 1961 to 1994 be sufficient evidence, until the contrary is shown, of the facts stated therein, without proof of any signature on it or that the signatory was the proper person to sign it.

 22.—(1) Where a person is convicted of an offence under section 49 or 50 of the Principal Act or section 13, 14 or 15, committed after the commencement of this section, the court shall, unless it is satisfied that there are special and substantial reasons for not so doing, order the person to pay to the court a contribution towards the costs and expenses incurred by the Bureau in the performance of its functions not exceeding such amount as may, for the time being, stand prescribed. *Costs of prosecutions under sections 49 and 50 of Principal Act and Part III*

 (2) Payments under subsection (1) shall be disposed of in such manner as may be prescribed.

 23.—(1) In a prosecution of a person for an offence under section 13 for refusing or failing to comply with a requirement to provide 2 specimens of his breath, it shall be a defence for the defendant to satisfy the court that there was a special and substantial reason for his refusal or failure and that, as soon as practicable after the refusal or failure concerned, he complied (or offered, but was not called upon to comply) with a requirement under the section concerned in relation to the taking of a specimen of blood or the provision of a specimen of urine. *Defence to refusal to permit taking of specimen of blood or to provide 2 specimens of breath*

 (2) In a prosecution of a person for an offence under section 13, 14 or 15 for refusing or failing to comply with a requirement to permit a designated doctor to take a specimen of blood or for refusing or failing to comply with a requirement of a designated doctor in relation to the taking of a specimen of blood, it shall be a defence for the defendant to satisfy the court that there was a special and substantial reason for his refusal or failure and that, as soon as practicable after the refusal or failure concerned, he complied (or offered, but was not called upon, to comply) with a requirement under the section concerned in relation to the provision of a specimen of urine.

 (3) Notwithstanding subsections (1) and (2), evidence may be given at the hearing of a charge of an offence under section 49 or 50 of the Principal Act that the defendant refused or failed to comply with a requirement to provide 2 specimens of his breath, or that the defendant refused or failed to comply with a requirement to permit the taking of a specimen of his blood or to comply with a requirement of a designated doctor in relation to the taking of a specimen of blood, as the case may be.

Bar to certain defence to charges under section 49 and 50 of Principal Acts	**24.**—It shall not be a defence for a person charged with an offence under section 49(1) or 50(1) of the Principal Act to show that, in relation to the facts alleged to constitute the offence, an analysis or determination under the Road Traffic Acts 1961 to 1994 has not been carried out or that he has not been requested under section 12 to provide a specimen of his breath.

Appendix B

Road Traffic Act 1995

AN ACT TO AMEND CERTAIN PROVISIONS OF THE ROAD TRAFFIC ACT 1961 RELATING TO CONSEQUENTIAL DISQUALIFICATION ORDERS.

BE IT ENACTED BY THE OIREACHTAS AS FOLLOWS:

1.—In this Act— *Definitions*
'the Act of 1961' means the Road Traffic Act 1961;
'the Act of 1994' means the Road Traffic Act 1994;
'section 26' means section 26 (inserted by the Act of 1994) of the Act of 1961.

2.—Section 26 is hereby amended by the substitution for subsections (3) and (4) of the following subsections: *Consequential disqualification orders*

'(3) A consequential disquaification order resulting from a conviction for an offence under—
    (*a*) section 53 of this Act tried on indictment, or
    (*b*) section 106 of this Act, where—
        (i) the offence involved a contravention of paragraph (*a*) or (*b*) of subsection (1) of that section,
        (ii) injury was caused to a person,
        (iii) a mechanically propelled vehicle was involved in the occurrence of the injury, and
        (iv) the convicted person as the driver of the vehicle concerned,
shall operate to disqualify the person to whom the order relates for holding any driving licence whatsoever during a specified period and, unless the court is satisfied that a special reason (which it shall specify when making its order) has been proved by the convicted person to exist in his or her particular case such that it should not so operate, thereafter until the person has produced to the appropriate licensing authority, as may be specified in the order, a certificate of competency or both a certificate of competency and a certificate of fitness.

(4)(*a*) The period of disqualification specified in a consequential disqualification order shall, where the person to whom the order relates is convicted of an offence under—
        (i) section 49 of this Act consisting of a contravention of subsection (1) of that section,
        (ii) subsection (1) of section 50 of this Act,

(iii) section 53 of this Act tried on indictment,
(iv) section 106 of this Act, where the offence involved the matters specified in subparagraphs (i) to (iv) of subsection (3)(*b*) of this section, or
(v) section 13, 14 or 15 of the Road Traffic Act 1994,

be less than 2 years in the case of a first offence under the section concerned and not less than 4 years in the case of a second or any subsequent offence under the same section.

(*b*) (i) The period of disqualification specified in a consequential disqualification order shall, where the person to whom the order relates is convicted of an offence under section 49 of this Act consisting of a contravention of subsection (2), (3) or (4) of that section or an offence under subsection (2), (3) or (4) of section 50 of this Act, be—
  (I) in the case of a first offence under the said section 49 or 50, as the case may be, not less than the appropriate period specified in column (3) of the Table to this subsection, and
  (II) in the case of a second or subsequent offence under the same section, not less than the appropriate period specified in column (4) of that Table.
(ii) In subparagraph (i) of this paragraph, 'appropriate period' means the period that is appropriate having regard to—
  (I) the concentration of alcohol in the blood, urine or breath, as the case may be, of the person concerned in relation to which that person was convicted of the offence concerned, and
  (II) the concentration of alcohol in blood, urine or breath, as may be appropriate, specified in column (2) of the Table to this subsection.

Appendix B

TABLE

Reference Number (1)	Concentration of alcohol (2)	First offence under the section concerned (3)	Second or any subsequent offence under the same section (4)
1.	(a) Not exceeding 100 milligrammes of alcohol per 100 millilitres of blood; (b) Not exceeding 135 milligrammes of alcohol per 100 millilitres of urine; (c) Not exceeding 44 microgrammes of alcohol per 100 millilitres of breath.	3 months	6 months
2.	(a) Exceeding 100 milligrammes but not exceeding 150 milligrammes of alcohol per 100 millilitres of blood; (b) Exceeding 135 milligrammes but not exceeding 200 milligrammes of alcohol per 100 millilitres of urine; (c) Exceeding 44 milligrammes but not exceeding 66 microgrammes of alcohol per 100 millilitres of breath.	1 year	2 years
3.	(a) Exceeding 150 milligrammes of alcohol per 100 millilitres of blood; (b) Exceeding 200 milligrammes of alcohol per 100 millilitres of urine. (c) Exceeding 66 microgrammes of alcohol per 100 millilitres of breath.	2 years	4 years

3.—(1) Notwithstanding the provisions of subsections (1) and (1A) of section 29, where a person is convicted of an offence under— *Transitional*

    (a) section 49 or 50 of the Act of 1961,
    (b) section 53 of the Act of 1961, tried summarily, or
    (c) section 13, 14 or 15 of the Act of 1994,

committed on or after the 2nd day of December 1994, but before the passing of this Act, and the court has, pursuant to the provisions of section 26, made a consequential order operating to disqualify the person for holding any driving

licence whatsoever during—
> (i) a specified period, and
> (ii) thereafter until he has produced to the appropriate licensing authority, as may be specified in the order, a certificate of competency or both a certificate of competency and a certificate of fitness,

the person may apply to the court which made the order for a declaration that the order shall, to the extent, but only to the extent, that it operates to impose the requirement referred to in *paragraph (ii)* of this subsection, cease to have effect and, if that court considers that circumstances exist which justify such a course, it may make the declaration and, if it does so, the order shall cease to have effect to the extent aforesaid.

(2)(*a*) Notwithstanding the provisions of subsection (1) and (1A) of section 29, where—
> (i) a person is convicted of an offence under—
>> (I) section 49 of the Act of 1961 consisting of a contravention of subsection (2) or (3) of that section, or
>> (II) subsection (2) or (3) of section 50 of the Act of 1961,
>>
>> committed on or after the 2nd day of December 1994, but before the passing of this Act, and
>
> (ii) the court has, pursuant to the provisions of section 26, made a consequential disqualification order in respect of the person,

the person may apply to the court which made the order for a reduction in the period of disqualification specified in the order and that court, if it considers that circumstances exist which justify such a course, may by order substitute in the disqualification order, for that period, a period that is less than that period but is not less than the period that would have been the appropriate period specified in column (3) or (4), as may be appropriate, of the Table to subsection (4) (inserted by this Act) of section 26 in relation to the offence if it had been committed after such passing.

(*b*) In *paragraph (a)* of this subsection, 'appropriate period' has the meaning assigned to it by subsection (4)(*b*)(ii) of section 26.

(3) The provisions of subsections (2) to (8) of section 29 shall apply to applications under this section as they apply to applications under subsection (1) of that section.

(4) Where a consequential disqualification order has been varied under *subsection (1)* or *(2)* of this section, an application for the removal of the disqualification concerned may be made in accordance with the provisions of section 29.

(5) In this section, 'section 29' means section 29 of the Act of 1961.

Short title, collective citation and construction

4.—(1) This Act may be cited as the Road Traffic Act 1995.

(2) The Road Traffic Acts 1961 to 1994 and this Act may be cited together as the Road Traffic Acts 1961 to 1995 and shall be construed together as one Act.

Appendix C

The Doctor's Form

Form to be completed by a designated doctor under section 18 of the Road Traffic Act 1994.

1. Name and address of the person from whom the specimen to which this form relates was taken, or who provided the specimen.   _____
   _____
   _____
   _____

2. Nature of specimen. (insert 'blood' or 'urine' as appropriate)   _____

3. Place at which specimen was taken or provided.

   (delete whichever is not appropriate)

   _____
   (a) Garda Síochána Station

   _____
   (B) Hospital

4. Date on which specimen was taken or provided.   _____

5. Time at which specimen was taken or provided.   _____

6. Garda Síochána station from which the specimen will be forwarded to the Bureau. (to be completed in the case of a specimen taken or provided in a hospital)   _____

I, the undersigned designated doctor
   (*a*) took from the person named at 1 above the specimen of blood or (delete whichever is not appropriate)
   (*b*) obtained from the person named at 1 above the specimen of urine
to which this form relates.

I divided the specimen into two parts. I placed each part in a container, which I forthwith sealed. I labelled each container with the name of the person and the date. I gave both containers to a member of the Garda Síochána.

Signature of designated doctor   _____

The Bureau's Certificate

Certificate issued by the Medical Bureau of Road Safety
under section 19 of the Road Traffic Act 1994.

Particulars relating to specimen received for analysis, as shown on the form completed by designated doctor:—

1. Name and address of the person from whom the specimen was taken or who provided the specimen.

   _____
   _____
   _____
   _____

2. Nature of specimen. (insert 'blood' or 'urine' as appropriate)

   _____

3. Place at which specimen was taken or provided.

   _____
   Garda Síochána Station

   (delete whichever is not appropriate)

   _____
   Hospital

Appendix C

4. Date on which specimen was taken or provided. _____

5. Time at which specimen was taken or provided. _____

6. Garda Síochána station from which the specimen analysed was forwarded. (to be completed in the case of a specimen taken or provided in a hospital) _____

The Medical Bureau of Road Safety certifies that on analysis by the Bureau the specimen to which the above particulars relate contained a concentration of _____ milligrammes of alcohol per 100 millilitres of blood *or* urine. (delete whichever is not appropriate)

Signature of person who carried out the analysis _____

Date _____

This certificate is issued under section 19 of the Road Traffic Act 1994.

The Seal of the Medical Bureau of Road Safety was affixed hereto this _____ day of _____ in the presence of
_____

(Chairman *or* Director *or* Deputy Director of the Bureau *or* member of the Bureau duly authorised by the Bureau to act in that behalf).

Index

accused (*see* defendant)
adjournment
    does not cure failure to comply with basic requirement of natural justice 4.19
    may be granted by Circuit Court 9.04
    may be granted by District Court 8.09
alcohol
    consumption of to frustrate prosecution 2.20
amendment
    of summons 8.05-8.07
    power of Circuit Court to make 9.04
analysis
    manner of 5.05
    rendered false by unspecified substance 5.04
    whether carried out as soon as practicable 4.18
apparatus (*see* breathalyser and intoximeter)
    does not have to have been supplied by the bureau 4.10
    presumed to be one for determining concentration of alcohol in breath 4.22
    presumed to be one for indicating presence of alcohol in breath 3.05
    production of in court 3.09
appeal
    abandonment of in the event of a case stated 9.06
    documents required for 9.01
    generally 9.01 et seq.
    hearing of 9.03-9.04.
appellant (*see* appeal)
    may appeal against conviction and sentence or sentence only 9.03
    must be liberated on entering into recognizance 9.02
arrest
    an essential element 3.10
    at home or other private place 3.17-3.21
    elements of 3.14
    generally 3.10 et seq.
    justified by failure to pass breathalyser 3.08, 3.11
    opinion justifying 3.11
    procedure following 3.22
    upon an arrest 3.23
    what constitutes 3.16
attempt to drive (*see* driving) 2.11

breath
    apparatus for testing 4.22
    specimens of 4.22
breathalyser
    failure to pass sufficient to justify arrest 3.08, 3.11
    generally 3.05 et seq.
    no obligation to breathalyse 3.02
    production of apparatus in court 3.09
    significance of positive test 3.08.
bureau (*see* Medical Bureau of Road Safety)

case stated
   and abandonment of right of appeal 9.06
   generally 9.06 et seq.
certificate of the Medical Bureau of Road Safety (*see* form of designated doctor)
   effect of error in defendant's name or address 5.07
   essential proof 5.02
   evidential value of 5.02-5.04
   legibility of signature on 5.06
   not furnished despite requests 4.19
   not necessary to prove signature on 5.02
   signature of analyst to be placed on 5.05
   whether forwarded as soon as practicable 4.17 et seq.
certiorari
   circumstances in which it may be granted 9.10-9.13
   granted where complaint not proved 7.11
   granted where deliberate decision to withhold certificate from defendant 4.19
   where appeal pending 9.15
   where signature affixed by rubber stamp 7.14
charge sheet
   amendment of 8.08
   and the necessity for a complaint 7.23
   copy of must be furnished to the defendant 7.21
   lodgment of 7.21
   particulars of offence must be set out on 7.21
   procedure by 7.21-7.22
Circuit Court
   decision final 9.05
   judge may direct the issue of warrant 9.04
   jurisdiction of on hearing appeal 9.03-9.04
   may increase sentence 9.03
   may not quash District Court order 9.03
   power to amend 9.04
   right of appeal to 9.01
clerk (*see* District Court clerk)
common informer 7.01
complainant (*see* common informer, complaint and Director of Public Prosecutions)
complaint
   as foundation of jurisdiction 7.08
   cause of to be stated in summons 7.13
   challenged by defence 7.11
   does not have to disclose that it is made in respect of a statutory offence 8.14
   form of 7.09
   hearing and determination of 8.01-8.03
   proof of 7.11
   required for issue of summons 7.04, 7.08
   required where defendant charged on charge sheet 7.23
   time limit for 7.10
   variance between complaint and evidence 8.05-8.06
constitutional justice 9.13
conviction
   certainty in 8.15
   copy of must be produced on application for certiorari 9.14
   for statutory offence 8.14
   requirements of good conviction 8.14
   uncertainty in 2.09
costs 8.16
Courts (No. 3) Act 1986
   summonses issued under 7.15-7.17
Courts (Supplemental Provisions) Act 1961
   case stated under 9.07
Criminal Justice Act 1951 7.22, 8.11, 9.16

Index

Criminal Justice Act 1984 7.22
Criminal Justice (Administration) Act 1924 7.01
custody record 4.01

Davitt Commission Report 1.04
defects 8.05-8.06, 8.07
defence
  'hip flask' 2.20
  no defence that analysis not carried out nor specimen requested 2.03, 2.18
  to refusing or failing to provide breath specimens 4.22
  to refusing or failing to provide blood specimen 4.07, 4.09
defendant (*see* arrest)
  access to a solicitor 4.02-4.03
  admission of driving 2.09
  charged under s. 49 may be convicted under s. 50 2.02
  charged under s. 50 may be convicted under s. 49 2.18
  constitutional right to privacy 2.05
  consuming intoxicating liquor after commission of offence 2.20
  error in name or address on certificate or form 5.07
  examination of 2.06
  has right of appeal 9.01
  may be allowed to at large or be remanded 8.09
  not allowed to call witnesses 9.13
  not summoned 9.13
  not to be convicted generally of offences 8.15
  observation of 2.05
  onus of proving certain facts on 2.20, 4.18, 5.04
  presumed intention to drive 2.18
  rights of 8.02
  service of summons on 7.18
  to be offered container containing specimen 4.12
  to be sent notice of imposition of fine 6.03
  treatment of 4.01
  whether entitled to copy of doctor's form 5.08
delay 7.24
designated doctor (*see* form of designated doctor)
  and procedure with regard to specimens 4.10
  completion of form by 4.10-4.11
  must divide specimen 4.10
  presumption that a person is 5.10
  to take blood or urine specimen 4.06, 4.08
detention 4.14-4.15
Director of Public Prosecutions
  applying for case stated 9.06
  right to prosecute 7.01
dismiss 8.11
District Court (*see* District Judge)
  appearance before after arrest 7.22
  determination suspended pending case stated 9.06
District Court (Charge Sheet) Rules 1971 7.21
District Court clerk
  creation of office 7.05
  issue of summons by 7.04, 7.06, 7.15
  must send notice of imposition of fine 6.03
  superintendence of issue of summonses 7.16
District Court Rules
  amendment under 8.05
  hearing of cases 8.01
  non-compliance with 8.10
  reproducing provisions of Petty Sessions (Ireland) Act 1851 8.01
  summonses issued under 7.04
  variances, defects and omissions 8.05
District Judge (*see* District Court)
  acting without jurisdiction 9.11

District Judge (contd.)
    adjourning case 8.09
    appearance before after arrest 7.22
    conduct of trial 8.03
    dismissing complaint 8.11
    hearing and determining complaint 8.01-8.03
    issue of summons by 7.04, 7.09
    may abridge time for service 7.19
    may direct substituted service of summons 7.18
    may extend time for service 7.19
    may receive complaint 7.04, 7.09
    may refer question of law to High Court 9.07
    may refuse application for case stated 9.06
    may require attendance of person who effected service 7.19
    must ensure trial in due course of law 8.02
    signing summons 7.14
    striking out complaint 8.12
    power to adjourn 8.09
    power to amend 8.05-8.08
    power to remand 8.09
    taking of note by 8.02
disqualification
    ancillary 6.05
    consequential 1.01, 6.05
    may not be remitted 9.16
    not a punishment 1.22, 6.05
    operation of 6.06
    removal of 6.08
    suspended pending appeal 6.07
    types of 6.05
doctor (see designated doctor)
    evidence as to defendant's condition 2.05
    examination of defendant 2.06
    refusing to permit provision of specimen 4.09
    requirement by 4.06, 4.09
driver (see attempt to drive and driving)
    detention of 4.14-4.15

driving (see attempt to drive)
    admission of 2.09
    conviction for driving or attempting to drive or when in charge 8.15
    generally 2.09-2.11
    presumption of intention 2.18
    proof of 2.09
    proof of time of not necessary in prosecution for refusal or failure 4.04
    quality of as evidence 2.04
    time of 2.07
    what constitutes 2.10-2.11
drugs 2.21
drunken driving (see driving)
    constitutionality of offence 1.27
    failure to prove element in procedure 3.02
    four separate offences 2.01
    statutory procedure 3.01 et seq.
drunk in charge
    generally 2.17-2.19
    statutory procedure 3.01 et seq.

error on the face of the record 9.12
evidence
    advance notice of 8.04
    discretion in trial judge to refuse to admit 2.09
    that the defendant was under the influence 2.04

failure (see refusal or failure)
fine
    generally 6.01
    imprisonment in default of payment 6.01
    notice of imposition 6.03
form of designated doctor
    delay in forwarding 4.12
    effect of error in defendant's name 5.07
    essential proof 5.01
    evidential value of 5.01
    manner of completion 4.10-4.11

Index 145

form of designated doctor (*contd.*)
    not necessary to prove signature on 5.01
    to be completed by designated doctor 4.10
    to be forwarded to Medical Bureau of Road Safety 4.12
    use of duplicate 4.13
    whether defendant to be furnished with copy 5.08
frustrating a prosecution 2.20

garda
    administration of caution by 2.09
    delay in forwarding specimen and form 4.12
    evidence as to defendant's condition 2.04
    evidence in relation to vehicle 2.13
    may breathalyse a person 3.05
    may demand name and address 2.09
    may require a person to provide breath specimens 4.04, 4.22
    may require provision of blood or urine specimen 2.22, 4.04
    member in charge 4.01, 4.14
    must forward container and form to bureau 4.12
    must offer container and statement in writing 4.12
    must supply statements 4.23
    no obligation to breathalyse 3.02
    power of arrest 2.21, 3.05, 3.10
    power to stop 3.04
    prosecuting as common informer 7.01
    serving summons 7.18
garda station
    certificate to be forwarded to 4.16
    person brought to may be charged on a charge sheet 7.21
    procedure at regarding specimens 4.10 et seq.

hearing
    cases of summary jurisdiction 8.01 et seq.
High Court
    appeal to Supreme Court from decision on case stated 9.06, 9.08
    application to where case stated refused 9.06
    case stated to 9.06 et seq.
    granting judicial review 9.09 et seq.
    power on hearing case stated 9.06
    question of law may be referred to 9.07.
history 1.01 et seq.
hospital
    obligation to provide specimen in 4.08

imprisonment
    for non-payment of fine 6.02
    generally 6.04
in charge
    what constitutes being 2.19
information (*see* complaint)
informer (*see* common informer)
Interpretation Act 1937 7.10
intoxicant (*see* alcohol, drugs and intoxicating liquor) 2.21
intoxicating liquor
    no need to disprove consumption of after commission of offence 2.20
intoximeter 4.22-4.24

judicial review (*see certiorari*)
    generally 9.09 et seq.
    not precluded by finality of Circuit Court decision 9.05
    procedure 9.14
jurisdiction
    concept of 9.11
    declining of 9.03
    excess of 9.11

jurisdiction (*contd.*)
    of Circuit Court confined to limits imposed on District Court 9.04
    want of 9.11

Licensing Act 1872 1.01

mechanically propelled vehicle (*see* vehicle)
    what constitutes 2.12-2.14
Medical Bureau of Road Safety (*see* certificate of the Medical Bureau of Road Safety)
    as a body corporate 5.05
    establishment and functions 1.08
    form to be forwarded to 4.12
    may analyse one of two specimens 4.16
    must analyse specimen 4.16
    must forward certificate 4.16
    not required to ensure receipt of certificate 4.20
    procedure at regarding specimens 4.16 et seq.
    specimen to be forwarded to 4.12
    whether it has performed its duties as soon as practicable 4.17 et seq.

natural justice (*see* constitutional justice)
notice
    of imposition of fine 6.03

offence
    detection of 3.03
    minor 1.22
omissions 8.05-8.06, 8.07

peace commissioner
    establishment of post 7.05
    issue of summons by 7.04, 7.07, 7.15
    power to remand 7.22

penalties
    Circuit Court cannot impose penalty which could not have been imposed by District Court 9.04
    generally 6.09 et seq.
    in excess of that laid down by statute 9.11
Petty Sessions (Ireland) Act 1851
    provisions of reproduced in District Court Rules 8.01
    summonses issued under 7.04
    time limit under 7.10, 7.16, 7.17.
place (*see* public place)
Probation of Offenders Act 1907 6.09, 6.11, 9.01
procedure (*see* drunken driving)
prosecution
    frustration of 2.20
    not required to disprove distortion of analysis 5.04
    not required to prove that the doctor had used any particular equipment or that the equipment had been supplied by the bureau 4.10
    required to prove making of complaint 7.11
    required to supply certificate 4.19
Prosecution of Offences Act 1974 7.01, 9.06
public place
    administration of breathalyser in 3.06
    omission of reference to in conviction 8.15
    what constitutes 2.15-2.16

refusal or failure
    for a special and substantial reason 4.07, 4.09
    to comply with requirement 2.22, 4.04, 4.06, 4.09, 4.22
regulations
    judicial notice may be taken of 5.09

Index

regulations (*contd.*)
    providing for doctor's form and bureau's certificate 5.09
remission 9.16
requirement 2.22, 4.05, 4.06, 4.08, 4.22
road (*see* public place)
Road Traffic Act 1933 1.01
Road Traffic Act 1961 1.02-1.03
Road Traffic Act 1968 1.05-1.09
Road Traffic Act 1994 1.16-1.20
Road Traffic (Amendment) Act 1973 1.10
Road Traffic (Amendment) Act 1978 1.12-1.14
Road Traffic (Amendment) Act 1984 1.15

signature (*see* certificate of the Medical Bureau of Road Safety and form of designated doctor)
sentence (*see* penalties)
    appeal against 9.03
    Circuit Court may increase 9.03
solicitor
    access to 4.02-4.03
specimen (*see* analysis)
    analysis of 4.16
    delay in forwarding 4.12
    inability to provide 4.06
    intoxicating liquor consumed before taking of 2.20
    obligation to provide 4.04
    procedure to be followed in relation to 4.10 et seq.
    refusal or failure to provide an offence 2.22, 4.04, 4.09, 4.22
    to be divided into two parts 4.10
statement
    evidential value of statement stating alcohol concentration 4.24
    stating concentration of alcohol in breath 4.23
    may be tendered in evidence notwithstanding refusal to acknowledge receipt 4.24
    receipt of must be acknowledged 4.23
strike out 8.12
Summary Jurisdiction Act 1857
    case stated under 9.06
summons (*see* complaint)
    amendment of 8.05-8.07
    application for 7.16
    copy to be issued 7.14
    delay in issuing or processing 7.24
    form of 7.17
    formal requirements 7.13, 7.16, 7.17
    issue of 7.04-7.07, 7.09, 7.16
    lapse of 8.13
    must direct appearance of defendant 7.13
    must notify defendant that he will be accused 7.16
    must set out name and address and particulars of offence 7.16
    must state cause of complaint 7.13
    parallel procedure under Courts (No. 3) Act 1986 7.15-7.17
    procedure by 7.02 et seq.
    proof of service 7.19
    purpose of 7.02
    reissued 7.20
    service of 7.18
    signing of 7.04, 7.14
    substance of offence to be stated in 7.13
    time for service and lodgment 7.19
    two offences may be charged in one 7.13
    types of 7.02
    validity of summonses issued under Courts (No. 3) Act 1986 7.17
Supreme Court
    appeal to from decision on case stated 9.06, 9.08

tests
    co-ordination 2.04
    must be voluntary 2.04
trial (*see* District Judge)
    conduct of 8.03

variances 8.05-8.06, 8.07
vehicle (*see* mechanically propelled vehicle)
    disabled 2.13-2.14
    disposition of 3.24

warrant
    issue of not prejudiced by failure to send notice 6.03
    judge may direct county registrar to issue 9.04
    not to be issued where notice of appeal given and recognizance entered into 9.02